Scotland: Stunning, Strange, and Secret

A Guide to Hidden Scotland
The Hidden Gems Series

Christy Nicholas

Green Dragon Publishing

INTRODUCTION

Scotland, the name conjures visions of tartan covering every surface, hairy Highland cows, the deep glowing gold of a dram of whisky, perhaps even Mel Gibson in blue warpaint and a kilt. But beyond the tourist tat and the tacky gift shops, what is the real Scotland? What is the soul of the country, the hidden spirit that draws people back?

The Road to Skye

One's memories are unique, so each person is going to have a different image of Scotland in their minds. It may be the food, the people, the landscape, the drink, the history, the music, or a combination of all of these, that sings to a person's soul.

There is a wealth of fascinating things to do, stunning places to see, and friendly people to meet in the mystical Highlands. Like the colors of thread woven in a tartan, the aspects change with your perspective, and with time, to reveal previously hidden depths.

I have always had a special fondness for Scotland and Scottish customs. My great-grandmother was a McKenzie, so I knew I had a blood connection. I first visited in 2000 for a McKenzie Clan Gathering, a trip much too short. We've returned and spent time in the Highlands and the islands, Edinburgh and Inverness, the coast and the mountains. It is a place to be at home in front of the peat fire, eating your porridge, and drinking your dram.

In this book, I will explore many aspects of Scotland. I will delve into the history and myths that shaped the culture, as well as the superstitions and beliefs that still hold sway today. Parts of that are, of course, the ecclesiastic traditions, the Highland culture, and the various invasions from Ireland, Scandinavia, and England. I shall talk about the food, the music, the people, and, of course, the drinks. Some practical aspects to planning your trip, and your photography, are next, as well as some discounts and tricks to save some money. And, of course, a nice big section on hidden gems, places off the beaten track, to get away from the busloads of tourists and find your own special places.

Please, enjoy your journey through my book. And, if I have convinced you to travel to this incredible place, please let me know. I think everyone should visit Scotland and be enriched by this incredibly stunning, strange, and secretive land.

circa 8,240 BCE. These paint a picture of a population who moved around in boats from place to place, using stone and antler for tools.

The Mesolithic period, however, made way for the Neolithic period, as people settled down into permanent villages, and began farming the land. The stone house in the Orkney Islands called the Knap of Howar dates from circa 3,500 BCE.

One of the more spectacular remnants of the Neolithic people is a previously buried underground village in the Orkney Islands called Skara Brae. Dated to circa 3000 BCE, this is one of the few non-ceremonial ruins from that time, showing a domestic life not all that different from ours.

Skara Brae

Imagine living in these structures. The Orkney Islands are very remote, yes. They are also very windy and cold. We visited in June, and some days it did not get higher than 50° F. There must have been a very short growing season if they cultivated much at all. Most of their food would have come from the sea, some land animals, and foraging. The houses at Skara Brae were built underground, out of the raging winds and cold. They made bedsteads and shelving from long, thin stone planks, a central hearth fire, and tunnels to travel from home to home, to avoid the harsh winter weather outside.

HISTORY AND MYTH
What We Know and What We Believe

Prehistoric

Crossing into the land that is now Scotland, through the primor⊂ mists of history, the first settlers on the land came when the last glac i were retreating, about ten thousand years ago. At this time, it is belie⦈ that the land was still connected to continental Europe via a land bri⦏ that has since been flooded with the melting of the glaciers. Littl⊂ known about these Mesolithic people, but some have left their mark the modern landscape.

The Fairy Glen

There is a small encampment found near Biggar, dating to ⊂ 8,500 BCE, and the remains of a wooden house near Queensferry f⥾

This is also the time when stone circles and chambered cairns dominated the land, such as the Ring of Brodgar, the Stenness Stones, and Calanais Stone Circle on the Isle of Lewis. There are hundreds of these monuments around the country, some no more than ankle-high remnants of once proud and tall stones.

As the Bronze Age arrived around 2000 BCE, the natives started building hill forts, most likely for defense and domination. Eildon Hill near Melrose is one such example, and probably held several hundred houses. Smaller round houses of stone, such as Jarlshof and Sumburgh on Shetland, and crannogs built on artificial islands, were common.

Around 700 BCE, technology advanced and the Iron Age arrived; simple roundhouses began to replace the earlier structures. These were circular, built without mortar, and increased in complexity as time went on. They had a large, central pillar, sometimes elaborately carved into designs made to look like a tree. These evolved into the great circular stone Brochs, such as those found in Caithness and the Isle of Lewis. Brochs are drystone hollow-walled tower structure of a type found only in Scotland.

Pictish Cross Slab

Picts and the Roman Empire

Little is known of the people who occupied the houses and forts on Orkney, but the evidence we do have suggests they were fierce fighters, dedicated to their gods, and highly independent. Later accounts by the Romans, of course, painted them as cruel barbarians, and called them the

Pictii, or the Painted Ones, due to their tradition of using warpaint. This was not an unusual tactic for Roman propaganda, they often built up the image of their foes to make good press at home.

The Picts were an agrarian society, living in small communities, with cattle and horses being signs of wealth and prestige. Carvings show eagles, boars, wolves, hunting with dogs and falcons, and even women hunting on horseback. Their normal crops included wheat, barley, oats, and rye, as well as cabbage, onions, leeks, turnips, and carrots. Garlic, nettles, and watercress flavored their dishes. Wool and flax were common clothing materials. Fish, seals, and whales were hunted for food.

They were known among themselves as the Catuvallanii (the people of the cat), the Damnonii, the Epidii (the people of the horse), the Veniconea, the Novantae, the Caerinii (the sheep folk), the Smertae (the smeared people), and many other names which have disappeared in the mists of time. These names usually came from the tribes themselves, but then given a Roman flavor.

They were a unique society, a prehistoric people who survived into current times through myth, legend, and artifacts left behind.

The Romans attempted to conquer eighteen different tribes they had listed in Scotland. Circa 71 CE, the Roman governor, Quintus Petillius Cerialis, had launched an invasion into the territory, and General Agricola is said to have pushed his troops to the River Tay. When the positions won became untenable, the Romans pulled back to what is now known as Hadrian's Wall.

Glen Ogle Viaduct

While few Roman citizens lived beyond this line in the sand, they lived in constant danger of the Pictii. The wall was the first time the Roman Empire had declared an end, even temporarily, to their outward expansion, and may have been the first signal of its eventual contraction.

The Romans tried once more to conquer the lands, making it as far as the Firth of Clyde, where they built the Antonine Wall. However, it was overrun and soon abandoned in circa 160 CE.

After the Roman withdrawal, four tribes gained dominance in Scotland. In the east, the Picts held sway over the land from the River Forth and Shetland. They were known as the Kingdom of *Fortriù*, and likely had their seat at Menteith or Strathearn. In the west, the Gaelic tribe of the *Dàl Riata*, having come over from Ireland, had their fortress at *Dunadd* in Argyll. The southern Kingdom of Strathclyde was of Brythonic ancestry, also known as *Alt Clut*, and held their seat at Dumbarton Rock. In the south-east was the kingdom of Bernicia, descendants of the Germanic Angle invaders. From this latter kingdom came the Anglo-Saxon kings of Northumbria.

Dun Carloway

There are some interesting historical fiction/fantasy books written about the Pictish king Bridei by Juliet Marillier, and it is well worth the read if you are interested in this mysterious race. While we do not have much direct evidence of their lifestyle, the novels show a people with a great respect for the Gods, for hospitality, for the wisdom of the elderly, and the creations of their skilled artisans. They held wells and rivers sacred, and carved stones with curvilinear designs, which if you've ever tried to work with stone, you will know is NOT easy. Some aspects of their religion (in Marillier's books, at least) are very dark to our modern-day sensibilities. I believe them likely in the Bronze and Iron Age beliefs, as there are dark aspects of the world that could not otherwise be explained.

While they were likely closely related, the Picts and the Gaels were separate groups. The Gaelic kingdom of Dàl Riata was founded in the 6th century in the west of Scotland. It was close to this kingdom that the Irish priest and missionary Columba came, having been exiled from his native land by his brother, the king. He founded the first Scottish Christian community at Iona, and it still stands today as a spiritual retreat.

Keep in mind that what we know of history is cobbled together from myths, legends, scraps of verifiable historical data, archaeology, and studies of particular groups. Sometimes they don't mesh with each other.

Legends relate that settlers from Greek Asia Minor sailed the seas, and arrived in Ireland at *Cruachan Feli,* the "mountain of Ireland."

After some time, the tribe of the *Scotii* crossed the Irish Sea to invade Caledonia, north of Roman Britain, and settled in Iona. Supposedly, the tribe had been named after Scota, the Egyptian wife of a Spartan commander *Nèl.* This is just one of several legends behind the Gaelic invasion of the land of the Picts. Sometimes Scota is described as being the sister of the Egyptian Pharaoh, Tutenkhamen.

While the Picts did try rejecting Gaelic and Christian influence, it eventually took over, and the Picts intermarried with the Gaels to become the Scots. The Scotii were one of the Irish tribes that came over during that time, and they gave their name to the land. Their union was a result, ultimately, to the incursions of the Vikings from all sides and the Saxons that came up from the south, they combined to fight, forming the Kingdom of Scotland.

There is a fascinating book by Bryan Sykes, called *Saxons, Vikings, and Celts: The Genetic Roots of Britain and Ireland*. The book explores the DNA evidence of settlement and invasion by the various groups into Scotland, Ireland, England, and Wales, and comes to some fascinating conclusions about these invasions.

The Kingdom of Scotland

The first king was *Cìnaed mac Ailpìn* (Kenneth McAlpin), due to a merger between the Gaelic and Pictish lines circa 840 CE, though his line was disputed throughout many successions. After Kenneth passed on, his successors, *Màel Colùm I* (Malcolm I) and *Màel Colùm mac Cinàeda* (Malcolm II), helped solidify this kingdom. The arrival of Constantine II, who retired as a monk in St. Andrews, may have helped Christianize the kingdom, and kept the Celtic Christianity in line with Roman beliefs.

The last of his line was Malcolm II, who died in the early 11th century, passing the kingship on to his daughter's son, Duncan I (of Macbeth fame), known as the head of the House of Dunkeld. According to Shakespeare, Duncan was killed by Macbeth, who was then overthrown by *Màel Coluim III*, Duncan's son.

However, the Bard was a playwright, not a historian. Relying upon his account of events isn't always the best choice.

Màel Coluim III, also known as *Ceann Mòr* (Great Chief), was the man who brought stability and power to the House of Dunkeld. He had many descendants, and, despite the frightening tendency for them to kill each other, established a dynasty that lasted two hundred years.

However, his second marriage, to the Anglo-Hungarian Princess Margaret, prompted William the Conqueror to invade Northumbria. Màel Colùm submitted, which opened later claims over Scotland by the English crown.

One of his successors, David I, started what was called the Davidian Revolution. This was due to his upbringing as an English Baron, and his love of English and French ways of life. The Scottish traditions and institutions were slowly replaced, and members of the Anglo-Norman nobility took places in the Scottish aristocracy. He introduced feudal land tenure and knights' service, as well as a tradition of castles and cavalry. He created royal burghs, facilitated economic development throughout the country, and helped bring Scotland's structure in line with other nearby countries.

These reforms were continued by David I's heirs, until Alexander III in 1286. When Alexander III died, the only heir of the line who remained was his infant daughter: Margaret, the Maid of Norway.

There is the tragic story about Margaret, this young heiress to a disputed throne; she was the one person who would save them all from civil war and unrest. While sailing to Scotland to be installed in her kingdom, her ship was tossed by storms and driven off course. Shortly after it landed in St. Margaret's Hope in South Ronaldsay, Margaret died. It is thought she died from the effects of seasickness, aged eight. When Margaret died, the nobles of the land asked Edward I for his advice on which of the fourteen rivals should rule. After choosing John Balliol as the successor, Edward I then claimed Scotland was now a feudal dependency of England.

Edward I used this as a wedge into which he tried sending troops to conquer Scotland. After John Balliol set up an alliance with France (known as the Auld Alliance), Edward invaded Scotland and deposed King John. The movie, *Braveheart*, focuses on this time in history. While the movie is not very historically accurate, the fact is that Edward I, known as the Hammer of the Scots, did not succeed in his quest to conquer Scotland, due in a great part to the work and patriotism of William Wallace, and Edward wasted considerable time and power in the attempt.

After the time of William Wallace and Edward I, the rule of Scotland went to Bruce I, aka Robert the Bruce. While he was crowned in 1306, he didn't have clear mandate until a decisive win against Edward II in 1314, at the Battle of Bannockburn.

In 1320, The Declaration of Arbroath was written by the victors and sent to Pope John XXII, a stirring and ringing statement that claimed *"...for, as long as but one hundred of us remain alive, never will we on any conditions be brought under English Rule. It is in truth not for glory, nor riches, nor honours that we are fighting, but for freedom, for that alone, which no honest man gives up but with life itself."* This document still rings true and proud among many of the Scottish people today, much as the Declaration of Independence does with Americans. Indeed, many think that the American document was fashioned, in part, after the Scottish declaration.

Subsequent attempts of Edward III to subjugate Scotland failed, and he lost interest when the Hundred Years' War with France started.

Glenfinnan Monument

The House of Stuart

After David II, the last of the Bruce line, passed in 1371, the first of the Stewart (Stuart) kings, Robert II, came to the throne. Due to infighting and mysterious deaths, his son, Robert III, sent his son, James I, to France for safety. He was captured by the English, though, and held for eighteen years. In the meantime, James' father died, leaving regents to rule Scotland in James' absence. When James I finally returned, he asserted his authority, executed several people who opposed him, and succeeded in centralizing crown control. However, this draconian behavior, while good for the realm, was bad for his popularity, and he was assassinated.

A couple generations later, James III married Margaret of Denmark, acquiring the Orkney and Shetland Islands as a dowry. This marked the passing of the islands from Norse rule into Scottish rule. While the islands are Scottish, they retain much of their Nordic feel and many of the place names still retain their Norse spelling. Even the English spoken there has a musical Nordic lilt.

James' son, James IV, then married Margaret Tudor, laying the groundwork for James VI to inherit the English crown in the 17th century. During James IV reign, there was much educational reform and creation of institutional infrastructure. It created a cultural renaissance which is still felt to this day.

In support of the Auld Alliance, when France was attacked by Henry VIII, James IV invaded England. He was killed in the Battle of Flodden Field, along with many of his nobles. This battle was commemorated with the traditional and very poignant song, *Flowers of the Forest*. The heir, James V, was an infant, and in control of the regents.

James V wasn't an incredibly effective monarch, and he made two marriages to French noblewomen, Madeleine of Valois and Marie of Guise. He died after another disastrous campaign into England, but not before he was brought news of an heir. This daughter would become the infamous Mary, Queen of Scots.

Much has been written of this ill-fated Queen, and I shall only touch on the highlights here. There is an excellent historical fiction novel written by Phillipa Gregory on her life, her loves, her many poor decisions, and eventually her tragic death.

She was raised mostly in France, betrothed to the *Dauphin* (heir) of that country.

Her mother, Marie of Guise, acted as Regent in Scotland, though in an unofficial manner. She did rally the Scottish and French troops against the English occupation and managed to eject them from the country. While there was trouble brewing between the Protestant and Catholic factions in the country, Marie of Guise did promote French culture and manners in the Scottish court. Again, this had repercussions for many years, both for good and for ill.

When Marie died in 1560, the Auld Alliance fell apart, and the Scottish Reformation abolished Catholicism in Scotland. Of course, the young heiress, Mary, was raised as a Catholic in France, and had married the Dauphin of France. Unfortunately, she was widowed at nineteen, and came to Scotland to take up her crown.

She was circumspect in her religion and did not force her beliefs on her now Protestant nation. However, this not only angered the Catholic nobles, but it was not accepted by the Protestant subjects, either. Her short reign of six years was a series of crises, intrigue, poor decisions, and betrayal. She was tricked into marrying a useless courtier, Lord Darnley. He angered the court with his extravagances and lack of propriety. Her Italian Catholic secretary, Riccio, was murdered; shortly thereafter, her second husband, the ineffectual Lord Darnley, was also murdered. She was then kidnapped by, and then either eloped or was forced into marriage to, the Earl of Bothwell.

In addition, Mary had been associated with an assassination plot against Elizabeth I and never informed her cousin of this plot.

This led to her imprisonment, abdication, and long exile at the hands of Elizabeth I, her cousin. In the end, after many lonely years of imprisonment, she was executed as a Catholic martyr.

The Protestant Revolution was a particularly strict movement under the teachings of both Martin Luther and John Calvin. The survivor of a massacre in France, John Knox, emerged as a leader of the movement and managed to convert most of the lowlands. The Highlands and islands mostly remained Catholic, except for those isles known as the "Wee Free Islands."

When the Protestant James VI succeeded the deposed Queen Mary, and many years later became the heir of Elizabeth I of England, he united the two kingdoms in 1603. It was after this time that the Scots settlement of the Ulster province in Northern Ireland began, starting a long war between the Protestant Anglo-Scots and the Catholic Irish they supplanted.

This dynasty was interrupted due to Charles Stuart, Charles I, and his mismanagement of the crown and the dichotomy of his mixed-religion countries. The people of England rebelled and started the English Civil War.

When the Royalists lost, the rebels beheaded the king and placed a Republic in his stead. This period is known as the Wars of the Three Kingdoms, as there were also revolts in Ireland and Scotland at this time. In Scotland, the Covenanters (the strict Protestants) governed and assisted those opposing the king in England. They were opposed by an army of Highlanders and islanders, led by Alisdair MacDonald, and this started the Scottish Civil War in 1644. Inexplicably, he abandoned his successes against the Covenanters, and they had the victory and established the Commonwealth.

After Oliver Cromwell ruled this Commonwealth, he invaded both Scotland and Ireland to cement his subjugation over these lands. He gained a reputation for ruthlessness in Ireland but died without a strong leader in England to take his place.

And, though he died of a disease, he was so detested by the people that they gave his corpse a public execution.

At that point, Charles I's son, Charles II, was asked to come back to the crown. The Stuart line was once again in charge of both Scotland and England.

It was not to last, however; Charles II's son, James VII/II, was Catholic, and this just made matters more heated and contentious between the Catholics and Protestants of all nations under his rule. He made it worse by placing Catholics in key positions and alienating his Protestant subjects with unpopular laws against their worship practices. His daughter, Mary, was a Protestant, and the wife of William of Orange of the Netherlands, and this seemed the best solution to the Protestants.

The Revolution of 1688, aka the Glorious Revolution, forced James to flee, and William and Mary were invited to rule the Union. This restored Presbyterianism, and abolished the bishops, though William tended to be more tolerant than many of his predecessors. In addition, they made it illegal for any member of the royal family to be Catholic without special permission.

Despite this solution, there were still many supporters of the Stuart line, and for several generations, the Jacobite (from *Jacobus*, the Latin name for James) Revolutions of the next century flared up. The first one was led by John Graham, and a group of Highlanders at the Battle of Killiecrankie in 1689 but was defeated.

In the aftermath of this resounding defeat, a tragic misunderstanding and heavy- handed retribution resulted in the Massacre of Glencoe, between the MacDonalds and the Campbells.

In 1707, the Act of Union brought England and Scotland together as one economic and political unit, allowing greater trade, and replacing Scottish systems of currency, taxation, and laws.

The Jacobites

This move was unpopular in Scotland, of course, and the Jacobites rose again, under James VII of Scotland (aka James II of England)'s son, James Frances Edward Stuart, aka "The Old Pretender." He had lived in exile most of his life, and attempted several failed invasions, most notably in 1715. It was ruined by a failure of coordinated risings in Wales and Devon, lack of leadership, bad timing, and bad luck. By the time James finally landed in Scotland, he was told it was hopeless, and so he fled back to the relative safety of France.

Blackhouse Interior

If you would like a glimpse into what life may have been like, watch the movie *Rob Roy,* starring Liam Neeson. Rob Roy was an historical character, though the stories of him are mixed. Some show him as a cattle-thieving rogue; others as a national hero, standing up to the oppressive evil English landlord. I suspect the truth is somewhere in the middle. The real Rob Roy lived near Balquhidder, and there is a small cemetery there, where his grave is situated.

In 1745, his son, Charles Edward Stuart, tried again to reclaim the Scottish crown. He was "The Young Pretender," or Bonnie Prince Charlie. The nickname Charlie most likely came, not from a diminutive of the name Charles, but from the Gaelic for Charles, *Teàrlach.* This rising was more successful, and he won some important battles, such as Prestonpans. Several clans joined the movement, albeit some very reluctantly. While he was successful at first, and managed to secure a good chunk of Scotland, he became greedy, and tried moving south into England. This overextended his resources, and many of his allies changed their minds. The rising ended with a horrible defeat by the Duke of Cumberland at Culloden. Charles fled to exile again, never to return.

If you ever visit Culloden field, please take the time to explore the visitor center. It has very poignant presentations on this time, this battle, and the events leading up to it. It is very moving, even if you have not a drop of Scottish blood.

The loss at Culloden broke the Highlanders and the Jacobites. What followed was a horrible part of British history, the Highland Clearances. In order to remove the teeth of the Scottish clans, the English outlawed Highland dress, custom, language, and capriciously stole from, killed, arrested, and transported thousands of Highlanders. These transportees ended up in Canada and America, often as indentured servants. Crofts were burned, cattle were slaughtered, valuables were stolen, and women were raped. Much of the land that was "cleared" of troublesome Highlanders was used for sheep, to support the budding wool trade in England.

Imagine living on a small farm. Life is hard, but peaceful. You tend your crops, your cattle or flock, and have enough to support your small family. There are, perhaps, four families within ten miles, also crofters. Your husband has gone off to a neighboring farm to help them with a building. Then the soldiers come, they slaughter the cows you rely on for your milk, run your sheep off, trample your crops, perhaps even salting the ground. They tear the door off its hinges and violate you and your daughters. They leave, taking everything they think might be valuable… and you have no one you can complain to, for they are the Crown's troops. You must either find a way to survive, leave, or perish. It was a very dark time, though many have managed to remain to this day.

There is a wildly popular series of historical fiction called *Outlander*, by Diana Gabaldon, also made into a television series. While it is fiction, it gives an excellent account of this time in the first two books of the series. You get to meet Charles as a historical character, as well as many of the Highlander Clan Chiefs of the day. You read about the conditions of the army, including a detailed description of the Battle of Culloden itself, and much of the aftermath. For more movie and literary places in Scotland, please see that section in *Ceilidhs and Flings*.

Many of the Highlanders were arrested after Culloden and ended up either dying in prison or being transported. Others ended up in America, Canada, and Australia, where they did their best to begin their lives again. Many of them were crofters. Others were fishermen and did well in coastal regions. Some ended up fighting in the American Revolution, thirty years later, some on the American side, some on the British side.

Lowlanders had it easier, partly due to religion and partly due to politics. Most of the lowlanders were Protestants and supported the King of England, so took up positions of power in politics and business, as well as in the military and colonial enterprises. This helped bring Scotland into the realm of a world trading power. The Scots developed a reputation of being fierce soldiers in the British Army, not only in WWI and WWII, but other wars, such as the Crimean, Napoleonic, Indian, and Boer Wars.

The Enlightenment

In the 18th century, a transformation occurred, taking Scotland from a poor, rural, agricultural society to a leader in modern industry. Glasgow and Edinburgh were the chief leaders of this transformation, using the tobacco, textile, and sugar trades, as well as The Enlightenment to increase the culture and wealth of the nation.

The previously created education system developed into an excellent university system and helped foster what was known as The Enlightenment in France. Philosophers such as Thomas Hobbes, David Hume, and economist Adam Smith, became leading speakers and authors of the day. Smith's book *The Wealth of Nations* is still being used today in Economics classes. And I know, because I had to read it!

A good banking system was set up in Scotland to deal with the burgeoning trade, especially in linen, and this structure stood them in good stead throughout the American Revolution and the shift in industrial needs.

Edinburgh

The beliefs of the Scots continued to fragment into the Protestant Church of Scotland in the Lowlands and the rather pagan-tinged Catholicism of the Highlands and the Islands, mostly the Gaelic-speaking areas. Later, the Free Church of Scotland formed, closer to the strict beliefs of the Covenanters of an earlier era, and very accepting of Gaelic language and culture. This has grown much in the Highlands and Islands. On some of the Hebridean Islands, known as "Wee Free" islands, businesses are closed on Sundays to this day, no pubs, no grocery stores, no shops; nothing is open on this day of rest. T

The greats of Scottish literature appeared at this time, such as Robert Burns, best known for *Auld Lang Syne*; Sir Walter Scott of *Ivanhoe* fame; and Robert Louis Stevenson, with *Kidnapped* and *Treasure Island*.

Burns is widely regarded as Scotland's national poet, and typically wrote in Scots dialect, which is a mixture of the older Anglo-Saxon Germanic language and Scots Gaelic; sort of a first cousin to modern English.

In other areas, the arts started playing a more important role in Scottish society. The Celtic Revival and Art Nouveau helped this, and architects such as Charles Rennie Mackintosh and his painter wife, Margaret MacDonald, reinvented the style of the age.

Glen Coe

Industrialization

Growing from the primacy of the linen trade in the 18th century, Scotland became a world center for engineering, ship building, and locomotive production in the 19th century, first with iron and then on to steel. Even today, the rail system in Great Britain is useful and well-maintained. This transportation system allowed Scottish products to easily make it to London markets, where Aberdeen Angus beef gained a world-class reputation.

Coal mining was huge and helped fuel the British Empire. By 1914, there were a million coal miners in Scotland, giving a stereotype of rough, brutish, isolated serfs. Industrialization took over from the southwest to the northeast, and Glasgow became known as the "Second City of the Empire," after London. Housing in the city became paramount, and overcrowding became endemic. This overcrowding also led to the formation of the first municipal fire brigade, in Edinburgh.

This period also saw a resurgence of love for the Highland culture, assisted by Queen Victoria's love of the Highlands. Her purchase of a "wee house" at Balmoral, adoption of the tartan in the Highland regiments, and the resurgence of Celtic ideals in literature and art helped all this along. After King George IV wore one on his visit to Scotland in 1822, kilts were suddenly fashionable again. This was the beginning of clans being identified by certain patterns of tartan, despite claims of an earlier correlation.

Ardvreck Castle

What few people know is that the Highlands also had a potato famine in 1846, as Ireland did. The difference is in the response of England to the crisis. In Ireland, the English landlords continued to ship out all the foodstuffs, leaving the Irish to starve or emigrate. In Scotland, the farmers were given emergency relief measures to keep the people from starvation.

What was life like for a 19th century Scottish crofter? His diet would typically be of potatoes, herring, oatmeal, and buttermilk and milk straight from the heifer. He would work the land for his landlord, and usually be able to grow enough for his rent, with a bit left over to feed his small family. He was likely still Catholic, but had a strong belief in the Other World, the world of the Fairies. He would likely be illiterate, and perhaps only speak Gaelic. He would live in a blackhouse, a crofter's hut made of stone with a thatched roof and was shared between the family and the few animals they kept. The hut could be very smoky with the peat fire inside, and smell, but one benefit of having animals indoors was in keeping the room warmer, especially in colder seasons. And a poor crop would likely result in eviction if the tenant couldn't pay their rent.

While the population grew with the industrialization in the 19th century, it contracted again in the turn of the 20th, with about two million people migrating to North America and Australia, about 30% Scotland's total population. These migrations ended only with the Great Depression, as no jobs were available abroad, and the vestigial wartime industry in Scotland offered some hope of employment.

Italian Chapel
Ornkey

The 20th Century

The advent of both World Wars showed that Scottish soldiers were still forces to be reckoned with. They continually showed their merit, with a reputation for fierce recklessness and lack of fear in battle. They wore their kilts and played their bagpipes proudly. And it may just be that, perhaps, their love of whisky, shared with their fellow troops, was behind the resulting growth in that industry after the war.

In World War I and II, Orkney played a major part, being an important Royal Naval Base, with shipyards and heavy engineering works in place. It was attacked several times by bombers, and, fearing submarine attacks, Winston Churchill deliberately sunk several ships in the water surrounding the entrance to the harbor, to limit access. These are called

The Churchill Barriers, and can be seen to this day, rusting away between islands in the archipelago. If you would like to visit them, you can see them along the line of islands that lead up to the Scapa Flow.

During World War II, a group of Italian POWs were held in Orkney. Hoping for a place to worship, they used a Quonset hut, and built a lovely little Italianate chapel, using paint to imitate tile work and iron scrap for the wrought iron works. It stands there today on Lamb Holm Island, a wonderful little jewel.

After war time, Scotland began declining economically and only recovered in the 1970s due to oil in the North Sea. Today, that oil is a big part of the Scottish economy, offering jobs and export income for the nation. Tourism and a growing awareness of their rich agriculture have helped tremendously.

In 1999, a Scottish Parliament was formed with devolved powers from the UK Parliament. Independence, however, remains a hot issue in politics today, and came for another vote in 2014. It failed by a narrow margin but will likely come up again in a few years.

Summary

Scotland certainly has a rich and varied history, full of drama, battle, mystery, and bravery. Perhaps they are more contentious than other populations, perhaps they just have a more recent war tradition than other cultures. The land itself plays a big part in the history of these people, offering barriers to invasion, growth, and prosperity. But still, it is a history well worth learning, to understand the background these people have, the proud traditions, the fierce, fighting spirit, the incredibly strong work ethic, and the unique ideas that help lead the world today.

What does this mean to the traveling tourist? It means that almost every square foot of this country, every rocky mountain, every mist-covered glen, every deep, dark loch, has a story!

You could plan your visit by theme, visiting the castle trail, or the whisky trail, or the Pictish stone trail. You could tour the Highlands and the Islands. You could travel around the coast by boat and hop from place to place. You could even rent a blackhouse on the Isle of Lewis and live like those at the turn of the century, with no electric or plumbing.

Do you find peace watching the sunset over the islands? Or stepping into a structure that's over five thousand years old? Would you be thrilled with seeing the soaring architecture of Edinburgh? Or the glistening granite in Aberdeen? Perhaps you prefer bird watching on the uninhabited natural islands of the Outer Hebrides. There's no end to the creative ways you can tour this wonderfully diverse country.

Calanais

SUPERSTITIONS AND BELIEFS

The world of myth is filled with fairies, creatures of mystery, curses, blessings, hidden treasure, and dark souls in the night. Every realm of creativity touches on these subjects, literature, film, music, art, dance, they all delight the mind and the imagination with sprites, goblins, and dark banshees.

Scotland's traditions are certainly no exception! Some of the tales and beliefs in the Scottish Highlands and Islands are shared by other groups of Celts, such as the fairies, others are unique to the Scottish pantheon of beliefs. While Ireland has a more cohesive set of these "fairy tales," there are several that were transported to Scotland's hills and glens with the Irish migration, and many that could be leftovers from the Pictish times.

I find Scottish myths have a darker theme than most of the Irish myths do. Perhaps this is because the country itself is a bit rougher in geography, less gentle in its mountains and coastlines. It could be because it has longer nights in the winter, being farther north. Longer nights meant more time inside, sitting around the hearth, so more time to tell stories. You wouldn't be idle while the stories were told, you could be spinning, or mending a harness, or whittling buttons, but you listened as the stories were told. No matter the reason, there are very few stories that are sweetness and light. Be gone the sugarplum fairies of Victorian lore; here are the Scottish tales!

Do keep in mind that the Scottish fairy beliefs, as well as modern pagan beliefs, are a living tradition. Please treat them with respect.

Am Fear Liath Mòr (The Big Grey Man of Ben MacDhui)

Also known (a bit more easily said) as the Grey Man, this monster, or possibly a spirit, haunts the mountaintop and passes of Ben MacDhui, the highest peak in the Cairngorm Mountains of Scotland.

He is said to be a very tall figure covered with short, gray hair, and causes hikers to be very uneasy even when they can't see him. There is some evidence of photographs of footprints and reports of sightings, but nothing concrete or provable.

While he is thought to be a supernatural being, he is also compared to Yeti and Bigfoot. In mainland Europe, creatures called *Wudewas* (Wood Men) have been reported back to the 13th century and are thought to be descendants of their Cro Magnon ancestors.

Hikers in the area have frequently reported they feel and hear someone following them, but the mists obscure any figure. One such report was by climber John Norman Collie in

1925, where he described hearing the crunching footsteps behind him in the mist, but with strides several times longer than his own.

Aos Sìth (Fairies)

These were the original pre-Christian divinities of Gaelic Scotland. The takeover of Christianity reduced these beings to hold only diminutive powers, also known as the *Tuatha dè Danaan* in Irish folklore. There are several different sorts of fairies in Scottish legend. Many people believe that some are angels that were leaving heaven, so when God saw the exodus and closed the gates, He trapped many of them on earth. Other sorts are believed to be the spirits of dead ancestors. *Aos sìth* are often bribed or mollified with offerings of food or drink, and care is taken not to insult or offend them. Many of their names were euphemisms to avoid angering them, such as "the Good Folk," "the Fair Folk," "the Good Neighbors," or *Daoine Sìth* (People of Peace).

Clava Cairns

The *Aos Sìth* often guard particular places, such as a hill, a hawthorn tree, a loch or wood. Dusk and dawn are particularly dangerous to encounter them, as are the feasts of Samhain, Bealltainn, and Midsummer (summer solstice).

There are many types of fairy creatures, such as the *Sluagh Sìth* (the Fairy Host), the *Cat Sìth* (Fairy Cat), the *Cù Sìth* (Fairy Dog) and the *Leanan Sìth* (fairy lover).

Arthurian Legends

While most of the tales of King Arthur took place in England and/or Wales, one of his traditional rivals, King Lot, was king over Orkney. King Lot had four sons who became knights of the round table: Gawain, Agravaine, Gaheris, and Gareth. Arthur's son, Mordred, was raised in his household. While there is little that we know for certain about these tales, there is no end to the variations, and many of them touch Scotland.

Bean-Nighe

A "washer woman" in Scottish Gaelic, she is seen as an omen of death. She can be seen near streams and pools, washing the clothes of those who are doomed to death, turning the river red with the blood.

Bean- Sìth/Sì

Related to the *bean sìth* of Irish legend, this spirit attaches itself to a family or clan and keens with the mourning of an upcoming death.

The Blue Men of Minch (also known as Storm Kelpies)

These odd creatures occupy the water between the Isle of Lewis and Scotland. They look for sailors to drown and stricken boats to sink.

Bonnie Prince Charlie & Flora MacDonald

When Bonnie Prince Charlie came to Scotland to reclaim his father's crown from William of Orange, he succeeded for a while, but was soundly defeated at Culloden in 1746. He was then forced into hiding and ended up on the Isle of Skye. He had relied on a faithful supporter, Flora MacDonald, to disguise him as a woman and smuggle him there, from where he could take a ship to France. The event inspired a song, still sung today, called the Skye Boat Song:

> *"Speed bonnie boat like a bird on the wing*
> *Onwards the sailors cry*
> *Carry the lad who is born to be king*
> *Over the sea to Skye"*

Boobrie

A mythical water bird of the Scottish Highlands, thought to be like the Great Northern Diver, but with the ability to roar.

Stirling Castle

Brahan Seer

He was a prophet, or seer, known to have the second sight. His true name was *Coinneach Odhar*, and some of his visions are thought to have come true. He foretold the Battle of Culloden, the doom of the Seaforth McKenzies, and the building of the Caledonian Canal. Perhaps his foretelling of "black rain" on Aberdeen was a vision of the oil industry off the coast of that shire.

Brùnaidh/Gruagach/Ùruisg (Brownie)

A good-natured, invisible brown elf or household goblin. They will only work at night, in exchange for a small gift or food, especially honey or porridge. If they are misused, they disappear. A small stool was often left near the fire for him. Some households had a "Brownie's Stane," or a small stone with a hole into it, where they would pour a bit of the

27

brewed beer for him. I find many similarities between this legend and the House Elves of Harry Potter fame.

Ceasg

A mermaid; half-woman, half-fish creatures. They are also known as *maighdean mhara* (maid of the sea) and have the power to grant three wishes to anyone who catches one. While there are some tales of sailors being lured to their death by these maidens, they seem to have a more beneficent demeanor than other cultures' tales.

Calanais II

Changelings

Sickly offspring of Fairies who are secretly switched in place of a human child. If you can see them with True Sight, they appear as little old men or women. The fairy child usually dies shortly afterwards.

Clootie

A Scottish name for a rag. The word cloot or *cluit,* perhaps referring to cloven hoofed animals or the Devil, though traditionally, a cloot is a strip of cloth or rag used to make clootie rugs and to patch worn clothing. These strips of cloth were also used to make clootie pudding, a type of steamed bread. The dough is wrapped in cloth then hung over simmering water to cook. This is likely where the term "Clootie Tree" comes from; a tree upon which people tie strips of cloth or rags that represent wishes or blessings, to be sent out as the fabric deteriorates. There are many Clootie trees around the British Isles, usually around holy wells. See the Hidden Gems section for more information.

Fachan

Also known as Peg Leg Jack, he is a creature with only half a body. He has a mane of black feathers, and a very wide mouth. Supposedly, he is so frightening he can induce heart attacks.

Fairy Flag of Dunvegan

According to legend, a chieftain of the MacLeods married a fairy woman, but could only keep her in a mortal life for twenty years. When she left, he chased her, hoping to keep her with him. All he caught, however, was her shawl. The shawl could be used by the MacLeods in battle to summon a fairy host three times. It has been used twice and remains on display in Dunvegan Castle today. I've seen it, in its glass case.

Ghillie Dhu

A solitary Scottish elf, guardian spirit to the trees. He is dark, clothed in moss and leaves, and is kind to children, but shy around adults. It's possible this is a remnant of the memory of Druids, the priestly class of the old Celtic religion. They were said to live in the trees, or at least worship in groves of oak trees.

Hauntings

Many of the ruined castles of Scotland boast a ghost or two. Some of the more well-known castles, with their hauntings, are:
- **Borthwick Castle.** Mary, Queen of Scots.
- **Braemar Castle.** a young, blond girl.
- **Castle Fraser.** a young woman murdered in the 19th century.
- **Cawdor Castle.** a lady in a blue velvet dress.

- **Corgarff Castle.** screams but no apparitions.
- **Craigievar Castle.** one of the Gordon family.
- **Culzean Castle.** a ghostly piper, and a woman in a ball gown.
- **Edinburgh Castle.** many, including a headless drummer and a ghostly piper.
- **Eilean Donan Castle.** a Spanish soldier, and Lady Mary.
- **Glamis Castle, Earl Beardie.** who plays cards, the Grey Lady, a tongueless woman, and many others.
- **Hermitage Castle.** My Lady Greensleeves.
- **Kellie Castle.** Anne Erskine.
- **Neidpath Castle.** a girl who died of a broken heart.
- **Skibo Castle.** a young girl.
- **Stirling Castle.** Mary, Queen of Scots, as well as a "Green Lady".
- **Tantallon Castle.** a woman who looks down from a barred window.

Kelpies

Kelpies are usually fresh-water creatures that occupy lochs and lonely rivers. They are also known as *Each Uisge* (Water Horse) and are sometimes associated with the Loch Ness Monster.

This creature appears to his victims as a lost dark gray or white pony, but with a mane dripping with water, perhaps with some seaweed woven in. If a person were foolish enough to ride on its back near the water, the water horse would take them down into the water to drown. Apparently, the rider is safe if there is no water nearby.

Once the rider is drowned, the water horse will eat him (except for the liver, which is allowed to float to the surface). They have also been known to turn into handsome men to lure women to their death.

The Legend of Robert the Bruce and the Spider

In 1306, Robert the Bruce became King of Scotland, but was immediately attacked by Edward I of England, forcing him into hiding. He hid in a cave on Rathlin Island off the coast of Ireland, and there, watched a spider spinning a web. He watched the spider try again and again before finally succeeding. This supposedly inspired Bruce to carry on fighting the English. He defeated Edward's armies in 1314 at Bannockburn.

Urquhart Castle

The Legend of Sawney Bean

Scotland has many tales of creatures, monsters, gods, and goddesses. However, some may have been human monsters. This particularly gruesome legend would make a great horror movie; a couple of books and horror films have certainly drawn on the legend.

Alexander "Sawney" Bean may have just been a creation in folklore, but the story has survived since the 15th century. Sawney Bean was the head of a criminal, cannibalistic family. Legend says he and his wife, along with their forty-six children and grandchildren, killed and fed on over a thousand people before they were captured and executed.

The family lived in a cave near Bennane Head (between Girvan and Ballantrae) for over 25 years. They had eight sons, six daughters, eighteen grandsons and fourteen granddaughters. The grandchildren were, supposedly, the result of incest. Not caring for "honest labor," the family ambushed, robbed, and murdered travelers, the bodies brought back to the cave, and eaten. The discarded bits washed up on nearby beaches and were noted by the nearby villagers.

When searching for the family, several innocent people were lynched; some were local innkeepers, being the last to see many of the victims.

One night, they ambushed the wrong man, as he was skilled in combat, and fought the family off long enough for a group of fairgoers to come by and see them. Now that the culprits were known, a manhunt was organized with four hundred men and bloodhounds. They found the cave, and the family was captured alive. They were taken to Tolbooth Jail in Edinburgh and executed without trial.

Much of this information comes from local broadsheets and diaries of the time, which are suspect, but kernels of truth may be the sources of the legends.

The Linton Worm

This legend dates to at least the 12th century. A great serpent that lived in a hollow on the northeast side of Linton Hill. A local Laird heard of this Worm, and its destruction of the nearby villages, and he tricked the Worm by jousting it with a flaming lance. The death-throes of the Worm supposedly created the odd topography of the region, now known as Wormington.

Loch Ness Monster

The Loch Ness Monster, or "Nessie," is probably the most famous of the beliefs of Scotland. She was first sighted by Saint Columba in the 6th century when the saint made the sign of the cross to keep the creature from killing him. The monster lay dormant for centuries, emerged again in the 1930s, and has been a tourist magnet for Loch Ness ever since.

Speculation on what this creature really is has run its course from a surviving dinosaur to a hidden time vortex below the lake. Many photographs (often proved to be fakes) have shown this creature, with a long, slender neck and humps showing above the surface of the loch.

Loch Ness is very long and narrow and surrounded by mountains. It is also very deep with black water, making visibility poor in the best of times. Although many expeditions have been launched to prove her existence, to date, none have succeeded.

Calanais II

Mòrag of Loch Morar

Like the Loch Ness Monster, this creature lives in Loch Morar, another long, very deep mountain lake, with only a short distance to the sea. Sightings started in the late 1800s and continued through the 1960s, many of them involving multiple witnesses.

Red Cap

Also known as the powrie, or dunter, this malevolent dwarf or goblin lives on the Scottish Border in the ruins of ancient castles. They murder travelers who stray into their homes, and dye their caps with the victims' blood, hence the name. They must kill regularly, for if their caps dry out, they die. The only way to escape is to quote a passage from the

Bible, which causes them to lose a tooth and leave. They are often said to appear as sturdy old men with red eyes and taloned hands.

Sir Rory Mòr's Horn

This is also in Dunvegan Castle. A new chief must drink a full measure of wine from this horn in one drink. The present chief evidently succeeded, in under two minutes!

The Scottish Play

Most thespians refuse to say the name of the Shakespearean play, Macbeth, for fear of black tidings and ill luck. I'm not certain why, perhaps because everyone dies in the play? Perhaps because Shakespeare wove a real witches curse into the story? Some say it began the night of the first time the play was performed, when an actor was killed with a real dagger which had been replaced for the stage prop.

Selkies

These creatures were able to take both seal and human form. The word for seal in Scots was *selch* or *selk*. Usually female, a human man could keep a selkie as a wife if he found and hid her seal skin. She would be a good wife and mother, and guarantee a fisherman an excellent catch, but if she found her skin, she would return to the sea, often taking her children with her. There are several films (mostly Irish) featuring with selkies, such as *The Secret of Roan Inish* and *The Seventh Stream*.

Seonaidh

A water-spirit who had to be offered ale to leave you alone. Perhaps they will sit and enjoy a pint with you after a long day of work?

Shellycoat

A Scottish bogeyman who haunts rivers and streams. He is covered with shells, which rattle as he moves. They are considered mostly harmless but may mislead travelers. They play practical jokes, like pretending to drown, and then laugh at the distracted would-be hero.

Stone of Destiny

Also known as the Stone of Scone and the Coronation Stone, this was evidently used by the kings of Dàl Riata at their coronations which they brought with them from Ireland. Around 840 CE, it was taken to Scone, where it remained until Edward I removed it to London in 1296. It was placed under the throne at Westminster Abbey until 1996 when it was finally returned to Edinburgh Castle. There are legends that it was originally used by Jacob in Israel, who brought it to Scotland. Other legends say that the Lia Fàil, a stone on the Hill of Tara in Ireland, is part of the same larger stone that the Stone of Destiny was cut from.

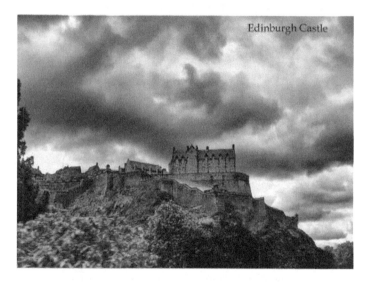
Edinburgh Castle

Thomas the Rhymer

Also known as Thomas of Eildon Hills, he lived on the Scottish Borders around 1300 CE. He met the Fairy Queen and dwelt in Fairyland for three years (some legends say seven years), though it felt like three days to him. Upon his return, he had the gift of poetry and prophecy, making his fortunes in rhyme. He is believed to have predicted the Union of the Crowns in 1603. Other legends say he asked for a gift to show he had been in fairyland, and the Queen gave him a tongue that could not lie, a distinct disadvantage for a diplomat or a courtier.

Wulvers

Good-natured werewolves, with the body of a man and the head of a wolf; they left fish on the windowsills of poor families and were particular to the Shetland Islands.

Most Scots figure that even if you don't believe in Fairy Folk, you shouldn't do anything that may anger them, and you should always keep an open mind as far as the other world is concerned. Iron or a Bible verse seems to be a rather universal charm against mischief. If you feel the need to calm an angry spirit, offer them a bit of fruit or a lovely flower. If you have lost something, a bribe and a polite request for its return often does the trick. Come to think of it, being respectful works for all sorts of folk, Fairy or otherwise, right?

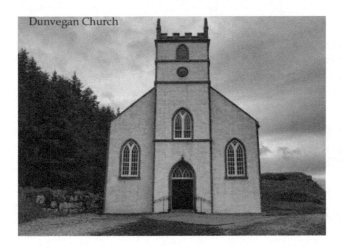
Dunvegan Church

GODS AND SAINTS

People of any age hold many things sacred. Holy wells, stone circles, a mountain top, a ruined church, the remains of a good man, or a piece of paper. Today's holy things may be family, money, status. But in the past, in the lands of the Celts, it's sometimes difficult to determine what was held sacred, and why.

This is because the Celts did not write things down very much. It wasn't forbidden, there are writings from Gaulish people in what is now France that date to 600 BCE, but it certainly wasn't common, or if it was, such writings have not survived. A tradition of writing didn't arrive to most Celtic lands until the Romans arrived, and for some (such as Ireland or northern Scotland), not until the Christians came to convert the natives. Stories were handed down within the families, told from grandmother to grandchild. They were cherished as histories and lessons and were held in a sacred trust. Kings had bards and historians who kept this sacred task, and who were able to call up a personal lineage or ancient tale from memory.

Most of the tales, legends, beliefs, and histories we do have were transcribed by Christian priests, usually well after the fact, and invariably colored with a Christian view on it. As a result, we have had to guess, through inference, outside accounts, and what little has survived the centuries, what the Scots held sacred. Many were also collected and published by various more modern authors, such as Lady Gregory and Walter Yeeling Evans-Wentz.

The advent of Christianity brought the tradition of recording beliefs, so it is easier to find the saints among the gods. But even then, local legend, politics, and missing records make holes and gaps in the accounts.

Regardless, Scots have traditionally held strongly, even fiercely, to their beliefs in the powers-that-be. Here are some of those powers explained or, at least, described.

Gods and Goddesses

Unlike Ireland, which is rich in the tradition of pre-Christian deities, Scotland has relatively few Gods and Goddesses to claim as its own. Many of the deities they do have are shared with other Celtic lands, such as Wales or Ireland. Often, we just have names, but no legends, no attributes, no details to flesh out the ideals that name was attached to. While there were plenty of fairies and spirits, deities were rather thin on the rocky ground, so to speak.

The Cailleach

The Cailleach

The one Goddess that does have some substantial lore about her in Scotland is the Cailleach, the hag-goddess, a winter goddess. The surviving tales could very well be a mixing of several separate legends from antiquity, some forgotten local deities, but she is deeply ingrained in the landscape of the land. Her name is found in many crags, valleys, and rocky places around both Scotland and Ireland.

The Cailleach is said to be a giantess who carries stones in her apron, and as she drops them, forms the mountains in the land. She is also part of a legend that says, on February 1st, she goes out to collect firewood. If the weather is poor, she cannot go to collect any, so she stays inside. This indicates that winter will be over soon, as she doesn't need any more fires that year. If the weather is fair, though, she goes and gets more firewood, and therefore winter will last another six weeks. Does this sound familiar? It should! It sounds remarkably similar to the Groundhog Day tradition in America and may have been its progenitor.

Glen Lyon has a small dry-stone house or shrine called *Tigh na Cailliche*, thatched and kept in good order. There are three stones inside, the largest of which is called the Cailleach, the second is the *Bodach* (old man), and the third is the *Nighean* (daughter). The legend of this place says that a couple of unnaturally tall stature came here one stormy, snowy day. They asked, and received, shelter from the weather, and decided to stay. The people built them a small house, and they had a daughter. While they lived there, the crops and livestock of the valley flourished. When they decided to leave, they made a promise that, if people remembered them, winters would be mild and summers would be warm. The people of the glen still tend this shrine today.

Other mentions of the Cailleach are on the Island of Shuna, where there are rocks called Cailleach *Bheur's* staircase, and in Moray, where there is a small loch called *Lochan na Cailliche*. Loch Etive has some stones called Cailleach *Bheur's Clacharan*, or stepping-stones. In Corryvreckan, there is a famous whirlpool in the straits between Scarba and Jura called the *Coirebhreacain*, Cauldron of Plaids, the tub in which the Cailleach washes her blankets.

Isle of Staffa

Fionn mac Cumhaill

There are several Irish legends involving Scotland, such as that of Fionn mac Cumhaill, a giant of a hero of Irish fame, who built the Giant's Causeway from Northern Ireland to the Isle of Staffin in Scotland. Both sides of this causeway have odd hexagonal basalt rock formations.

The story goes that the giant had a ladylove in Scotland and built this bridge to visit her. However, his girlfriend already had a suitor, *Benandonner*, and a big, ugly brute he was, too. So, fearing this rival, Fionn ran back to Ireland, dressed himself as a baby, and curled up to feign sleep. When Benandonner came over to see who this other suitor was, he saw the giant baby. Thinking it was a child of Fionn's, he imagined that Fionn, as an adult, would be so much larger, and ran back to Scotland, destroying the causeway as he did, to prevent Fionn from coming over in retribution.

Scàthach

Another Irish legend on Scottish soil involves the Irish hero *Cù Chulainn*. He was the warrior's warrior; unbeatable, incredible battle prowess, the strength of ten men, all that sort of stuff. He got his combat training from Scàthach, a warrior goddess who lived on the Isle of Skye, and ran a school for warriors, both men and women. *Cù Chulainn* had to pass several complex feats of physical and mental prowess before he was even accepted as Scàthach's student, but excelled at these tests, and proved his worth.

While he was there, he met another student, a warrior woman. Then he fell in love and had a child with her.

Athfhinn

Many place names could be derived from ancient deities, such as the river Aven in Banffshire, from the Gaelic Gàidhlig Athfhinn, meaning "the very bright one," supposedly referring to the wife of Fionn mac Cumhaill of Irish legend, who drowned in that river. Before her death, the river was called *Uisge Bàn*, or "fair water," a name not so dissimilar.

Other Gods

Many of the Irish gods and goddesses went to Scotland with the Gaelic invasion of the Dàl Riata in the period of 200 to 500 CE, such as the *Dagda*, *Macha*, the *Morrigan*, *Lugh*, *Balor*, and *Nùada*. I have visited a forest near Dundalk called the Hermitage, where there is an Ossian Hall (Oisín is the son of Fionn mac Cumhaill) facing a triple waterfall, three being a mystical number in many religions. Some other gods, such as *Taranis* the Thunder God, were common to many Celtic groups. Shoney was prayed to for good fishing, and the Sluagh Sìdhe was the Host of the Unforgiven Dead, riding the night skies. I've heard this legend in various forms, such as The Wild Hunt. Ireland and Scotland share many of their gods and legends since the people in both moved back and forth during the centuries.

Saints

Saint Andrew

It is widely thought that St. Andrew was born in Galilee, and that he and his brother, Simon Peter, were disciples of Jesus Christ. This helped him become the patron saint of Scotland (in 1320), as it was felt that he outranked St. Columba due to this relationship. He is also known as *Prōtoklētos* (first called) in the Orthodox Greek tradition. Legend has

41

it that several relics of St. Andrew were brought to the modern town of St. Andrews by a Greek man named Regulus to the Pictish King *Òengus mac Fergusa* in the 8th century CE. Another legend has the same Pictish King, during a battle, saw a cloud shaped like the saltire (white cross), and declared they were being watched over by St. Andrew. As a result, the saltire was adopted as a symbol and national emblem of the Scots.

There are several relics associated with St. Andrew, including his finger bones, a tooth, and a kneecap. These relics meant that the church of St. Andrews became a pilgrimage destination for medieval travelers, up until their destruction during the 16th century.

St. Andrew is the saint of many things and many places. The Greeks, Russians and Romanians hold him as patron. In addition, he is patron saint to women who wish to become pregnant, maidens, spinsters, and those with gout or sore throats.

Saint Adomnàn of Iona

St. Adomnàn was abbot of Iona in the late 7th and early 8th century CE, and the scribe that chronicled most of what we know of St. Columba. He was originally from Ireland but escaped with St. Columba to help found Iona. It is due to his writings that we know much of the history of this Abbey and the workings of St. Columba.

Saint Columba (Colm Cille)

Born in Ireland to a noble family, he was ejected from the country for ruling against his brother, the king, in a dispute. He moved to Iona in Scotland and founded a monastery there. Although there were Christian missionaries before this time, St. Columba is credited with bringing Christianity to the pagan Picts in the 6th century.

Saint David I, King of Scotland

St. David I was king in the early 12th century CE, becoming king at the death of his brother, Alexander, in 1124. When Stephen I ousted Matilda as heiress to Henry I, her father, St. David invaded England to help her to her claim. This war became known as the Anarchy, and it lasted for many decades. The war went on without him, after several abortive attempts, and he dedicated himself to his land and church. He founded five bishoprics and several monasteries, implemented several ideals within the church administration and within the Scottish government. The results of his many changes and reforms became known as the "Davidian Revolution."

Saint Filan

An Augustinian monk on the Isle of May, he left his native island to convert the Fife populace to Christianity. There is a cave in Cove Wynd (pronounced with a long I), Pittenweem, called St. Filan's Cave, with some rocks that are thought to be beds and a small holy spring. He is, oddly enough, the patron saint of skydiving.

Saint Magnus Erlendsson, Earl of Orkney

Related to several powerful Norwegian kings, he had a reputation for kindness and piety. Circa 1105 CE, he refused to participate in a Viking raid on Anglesey, Wales due to his religious convictions. He supposedly stayed on his boat and sang hymns instead.

He escaped to Scotland, but then returned to Orkney (which was then part of Norway) and disputed the succession of his cousin, Haakon. While they ruled jointly for a time, through the treachery of Haakon, St. Magnus was captured. Haakon made his cook kill St. Magnus with an axe, and the rocky area he was buried in became a green field.

Saint Mungo (Kentigern)

St. Mungo was a late 6th century CE apostle of the Brythonic Kingdom of Strathclyde who founded the city of Glasgow and became its patron saint. His four religious miracles are in the Glasgow City coat of arms. His miracles were: restoring life to the pet bird of St. Serf, restarting a fire with branches from a tree, a bell brought from Rome, and the retrieval of a ring from the River Clyde, by having a messenger catch a fish and finding the ring inside.

Saints of Lindisfarne:

- **Saint Aidan.** An Irishman who was a monk at Iona, he was also known as the Apostle of Northumbria, credited for restoring Christianity in the region. He founded the monastery at Lindisfarne and served as the first bishop.
- **Saint Cuthbert.** An Anglo-Saxon monk in the 7th century, he is regarded as the patron saint of Northumbria.
- **Saint Finan.** An Irish monk who trained at Iona, he became the Bishop of Lindisfarne, founding the cathedral there and converting two Kings of the Middle Angles, Sigebert of Essex and Peada.

Summary

Without a crystal ball, we cannot know, for certain, everything the ancient Scots and Picts held sacred. We can infer, we can guess, we can believe, but we cannot know. They seem to have revered powers that are attached to the land, the weather, the rivers, and the sea, forces that, to them, would have ruled their daily lives. A poor crop, a fierce storm, a bleak winter, any of these could spell out disaster and starvation for a poor crofter, living on the edge of a rocky island. Attempting to control this fate by appealing to a higher power would have been the only option given to them.

With the advent of Christianity, this power was consolidated into the Father God, but he had many saints, or appointees, to help those "on the ground." I find it interesting that many saints in Scotland were from the 6th and 7th centuries, when many of the people of Scotland were likely still pagan at heart and had probably just shifted their beliefs in name to one God, seeing their saints as modern incarnations of the gods and goddesses of old.

Many Christian priests appealed to the pagans by comparing their One True God with the pagan gods. One reason for December 25th being chosen as Christmas was to coincide with pagan rituals at Saturnalia and Winter Solstice.

Italian Chapel
Orkney

HIGHLAND HOSPITALITY

Traveler Tales

Judith wrote: I lived in Edinburgh for a while, and heard a story about the Edinburgh Acropolis. Edinburgh is known as the Athens of the North, and to honor their sister city, the clans decided to build a replica of the Acropolis on a hill overlooking Edinburgh. The story goes that they ran out of money before it was much beyond the pillar stage. However, it was told to me that the REAL reason that construction was never completed is that they were going to put a plaque at each pillar honoring each of the clans. But they were two pillars short and were unable to adequately resolve the difference, so work stopped and was never resumed. The shortfall may have been financial rather than based on clan pride, but the latter sounds far more like the folk I met.

Grampian Mountains

My own story: We had arrived at the second base of our trip, a small B&B in Grantown-on-Spey, near the Cairngorm Mountains. It had been a long drive through the mountains, windy and wet, and we were close to exhausted, but we finally arrived at our B&B, near the edge of town, Kinross House. It had plenty of parking on the wide street, and as we had six people and two cars, this was most welcome.

Our hostess, Jane, welcomed us with warm tea and biscuits, then showed us to our rooms. After we had settled in, she sat down and chatted with us in the sitting room. She gave us a recommendation for a local pub for some relaxing pints, and off we went, down the street to Craig's Bar.

The folks at Craig's were definitely characters! The mother (age 65-70) was planning on going off to China that summer to watch the Olympics. Most of her budget was for the flight, as she planned on flying Business Class. She wanted to have comfort on the long flight but planned on staying in hostels and camping once she was in China, to save money.

She shared some stories of her own, as well. We told her our next stop would be Orkney, and she mentioned she used to live and work there. She showed us the lovely jewelry they gave her as a going away present, one of Sheila Fleet's lovely designs; a round pendant with Ogham symbols and blue-green enamel work.

Kemberlee wrote: We had great experiences in Edinburgh. Upon arrival in Scotland, we booked a single night in a restored Georgian terrace house called Garland's. We didn't realize until we got there that it was a gay-friendly guesthouse. One of the owners, Bill, greeted us at the door in very tight shorts and a skin hugging tank top!

Bill was super. We asked about a local place for dinner, so he picked up the phone and was dialing the phone while pushing us out the door. "Don't you worry," he said. "Your table will be waiting when you get there." He gave us directions to an Italian place at the end of the road called Sorrento and off we went.

We walked in and two men rushed us! I wish I could remember their names, but the Irish owner was tending bar while the Scottish owner served tables (midweek so it wasn't TOO busy, but enough people to get the full effect of what came next). They both rushed us, arms open wide, calling out as they came forward, "Peter! Kemberlee! My God, my God, welcome!!" Hugs and cheek kisses for us both and more fawning as they showed us to our table, the whole while treating us like we were celebrities who had honored them with our presence. Everyone in the place started whispering and pointing at us. And it was like that for most of the evening.

It turns out Sorrento was owned by two best friends, one a Scotsman from Leith (just outside Edinburgh) and the other a man from Wexford, Ireland.

The next morning at breakfast, we were the center attraction as the only male and female couple in the place, and the other owner, Ian, fawned over us too. So, I asked in conversation how they came up with the name of the house, since neither were called Garland. Bill laughed and said, "Darling. It's for Judy!" (Judy Garland, one of the most revered gay icons.)

On the return visit to Edinburgh on the end of our trip, we had a couple nights in another guesthouse on the same road as Garland's (as it was booked out) called Abbotsford Guesthouse, owned by a lovely Scottish-Italian woman called Paola. Very accommodating and helpful with things to do and see around the city. She was full of stories and chat, and she clued us into the free shuttle into town across the road. It's not an official one, but since the coach company was located on the end of the road, they'll often stop and pick up passengers going into the city if you know where to stand! And since they're going that way anyway...

We had two nights at Abbotsford, and that meant two more nights at Sorrento. We walked in and both the owners stopped in their tracks and stared at us. Then we got a very shocked, "Oh...my...God! We thought we scared you away." They didn't know we were traveling after that first night and thought we'd been scared away. They fawned all over us again, but not as dramatically as the very first night. It was more like apologetic fawning, but in a typically humorous, Celtic sort of way. Indignant but not really, the kind with a, "You must have felt very put out to have gone through that. Oh my GOD!" Then big winks and a sly grin that warned us something else was coming. It was drinks, on the house!

On the final night, we went back to Sorrento and things were much calmer. Every other night it had been busy enough that they attended their diners yet always had a spare moment to drop over to see how things were going, and usually spend an inordinate amount of time telling us one thing or another. But this night they practically sat down to dinner with us. It was great. Such lovely people to chat with. Of course, "yer man from Wexford" was looking for news from home, too, and we were happy to oblige.

A funny add-on was each night for dessert, I had their bread-and-butter pudding, and each time I'd picked out the sultanas (raisins). That night, the Scottish owner didn't even ask for our dessert order since we ordered the same thing the previous two visits. He went to the kitchen and brought back a bread pudding... in a special bowl made separately just for me. No raisins!

When we finally were ready to leave, we told them it was our last night in the city and going back to Ireland the next day. I swear, it was like the parting of four of the best pals on the planet. I thought we were all going to cry. When I got home and started working with Scottish travel clients, I made sure they always had at least one meal in Sorrento and told them to tell the guys we had sent them. When the travelers got home, they emailed right away to tell us about the two insane guys in the Italian place.

* * *

50

Christy wrote: The Lodge at Edinbane has got to be my favorite B&B on our entire trip in 2008. It was wonderful! Large, rambling property, lots of rooms, a pub and dining room on property, everything run by Hazel, Pete, and Cal. It even had resident ghosties to keep you company at night. And yes, even though all the rooms on the website were pink, she had some purple, and even some blue rooms, available.

The pub had some wonderful meals. We had dinner there a couple nights, and breakfast was part of our B&B rate. They offered everything from cheese salads to beef bourguignon. One night, I had a lovely smoked mackerel salad, and it was quite strong!

The cheese salad does sound strange, but looked tasty, a nice salad of greens and veg with several different cheeses on it, including brie, cranberry Stilton, feta, etc. One evening, four of us continued to have drinks at the pub until almost midnight, out-waiting several locals who were shepherds drinking in the bar. One decided that he should start serenading us. It would have been lovely if we could have figured out what he was singing.

Hazel always wowed us with her breakfasts. She made Scottish pancakes for all, which are sweeter than the American version. She also served crystallized ginger preserve with them that was simply delectable, and very addictive. My friend, Kim, practically growled when we tried to take some of hers.

We had a couple of ghost encounters. Kim saw a shadowed figure in her room one night, though she felt no fear of it. It went away rather quickly. Jason heard a rapping on the closet door (which was right next to where I was sleeping). He looked for any reason for it, air vents, mechanisms, etc., and couldn't find a rational explanation for the tapping.

We were told that the ghost in that room was a rather prim Victorian lady, and if we told her we were married, she would stop complaining. Jason also heard a ghost dog walking across the hardwood floor in front of him. Now, he had been sipping whisky in front of the peat fire, relaxing that afternoon, and while the place had three dogs, they were all big dogs (Labradors) and all outside. This sounded like a small dog, click-clicking along right in front of him.

Hazel and her family made us feel so much at home that we will be back the next trip. And Skye is such a fantastic area that we can't help but go there again!

CEILIDHS AND FLINGS

When you think of Scotland and music, the first thing most people will think of is the bagpipes. However, while bagpipes are an integral part of Scottish music and national identity, there is so much more to the rich tapestry of Scottish music and dance.

While modern culture lumps "Celtic" into one grand mash, there are distinctive elements of some music that are Scottish, while there are some that are Irish, Manx, Welsh, etc. There are also many common elements between them. I believe it does the body of work a disservice to ignore either the differences or the similarities. I therefore see Scottish music as a subset of a greater, richer tradition of Celtic music.

Types of music

Classical

The Italian style of Baroque music probably came to Scotland in the 1720s, when cellist and composer Lorenzo Bocchi came to the country, and developed settings for lowland Scots songs. This was the birth of Classical music in this country.

He may have helped with the first Scottish Opera, *The Gentle Shepherd*, written by Allen Ramsey. Thomas Erskine, the 6th Earl of Kellie, was one of the more significant classical figures of this time, but his work was forgotten after his death, and is just now becoming rediscovered.

The 19th century saw the formation of the Scottish Orchestra, now the Royal Scottish National Orchestra. Sir Alexander McKenzie wrote several works for violin, piano and orchestra. Folk melodies have been developed for the orchestral performance by John McEwen.

A new concert hall has just been built in Edinburgh, in the St. Cecilia Hall. Movie scores by Muir Mathieson, Patrick Doyle, and Craig Armstrong have achieved international fame, while there is a Festival of Music every year in Orkney to celebrate the classical traditions.

Each year, the Edinburgh International Festival attracts some of the most influential musicians of the world, and Scotland itself has inspired many notable artists, today and in the past. One example is Mendelssohn, who wrote the *Hebrides Overture* in honor of his visit to the Outer Hebrides.

Folk Music

The earliest recorded non-religious music in Scotland was by John Forbes in 1662, "Songs and Fancies: to Thre, Foure, or Five Partes, both Apt for Voices and Viols." It was printed three times over the next twenty years. It contained seventy-seven songs, twenty-five of which were Scottish.

In the 18th century, many Scottish songs and tunes came into popularity, such as works by Robert Burns, Scotland's best loved poet, and works by Sir Walter Scott.

There are also many heroic ballads, poems, comical songs, and ancient songs. Of course, after 1745 and the collapse of the clan system, much of what was traditionally Scottish was banned by law through key laws such as the Dress Act 1746, the Act of Proscription 1746, and especially the Heritable Jurisdictions Act of 1746. All aspects of Highland culture, especially the Scottish language, were forbidden.

These traditions had to go underground until Queen Victoria discovered the quaintness of Scotland and, once again, made it safe to be Scottish and proud.

Revival

The 20th century saw a great revival of interest in the ancient Scottish songs and ballads, and many musicians helped to bring them back to popularity. Collections were published, like *Last Leaves of Traditional Ballads and Ballad Airs*, which helped inspire musicians into playing these tunes. James Scott Skinner, the first international star of Celtic music, became known as the "Strathspey King." Jeannie Robertson sang in Edinburgh, 1953, at the People's Festival.

American singers began to sing folk music, such as Woody Guthrie and Pete Seeger. This inspired some Scottish singers to do the same, such as Flora MacNeil and John Strachan. This led to the 1960s, and folk music got a new, more modern, veneer. The Corries, the McCalmans, the Ian Campbell Folk Group, Alex Campbell and Dick Gaughan played in pipe bands and Strathspey and Reel Societies. In the meantime, Irish folk bands, such as The Chieftains, helped make Celtic music popular around the world. Though Irish music became very popular in mainstream culture, Scottish folk music was still rarely heard on the radio or in pubs.

It was this environment into which musicians such as Andy M. Stewart and his band, Silly Wizard, and rock artist Donovan entered. Silly Wizard took folk music and made it cool and continues to be popular. While Donovan was a mainstream artist, he used Celtic influence in his albums *H.M.S. Donovan* and *Open Road*.

Jack Bruce, one of the founders of Cream, was also heavily influenced by his hometown of Glasgow mixed with jazz, folk, blues, and rock elements.

The Lone Piper

Another popular Scottish rock band, Runrig, from the Isle of Skye, has been going strong for forty years now, and has strong popularity in Scotland, the UK, Canada, and Germany. Other bands, such as the Whistlebinkies, Albannach, The Clutha, The Incredible String Band, Tannahill Weavers, Shooglenifty, and the Peatbog Fairies worked, and continue to work, in a fusion of traditional Celtic music with rock, bagpipes with electric guitars, drums, fiddles and harp.

One of the most poignant and heartbreaking songs I've heard was *Caledonia* by Dougie MacLean. It makes me cry from homesickness, though I've never truly lived in Scotland.

Popular

Perhaps Scotland isn't the first country that springs to mind when you think of pop or rock music. However, this country has certainly produced many notable talents.

- Annie Lennox of the Eurythmics came onto the scene in the 1970s and 80s and continues to make powerful music with her haunting voice.
- The Bay City Rollers was probably the largest Scottish pop act of the 1970s, in terms of sales.
- Sheena Easton who also went on to have a short-lived acting career.
- Many of the members of AC/DC were born in Scotland, including Bon Scott, Malcolm Young, and Angus Young.
- Simple Minds.
- The Jesus and Mary Chain.
- Big Country.
- The Proclaimers, of *500 Miles* fame.
- Julie Fowlis - her beautiful voice can be heard on the *Brave* soundtrack.
- David Byrne, Lead singer of the Talking Heads
- Gerry Rafferty, *Baker Street* and *Right Down the Line* being international hits.
- Al Stewart, Best known for his international hit, *Year of the Cat.*
- Leon Jackson, Won the X-Factor competition at nineteen years of age with his wide range and Michael Bublé voice.
- Primal Scream, Del Amitri, Travis, and many more.
- Rod Stewart, Probably *the* most famous performer in the world of close Scottish descent.

The Instruments

The Bagpipes

The bagpipe has long been an indelible symbol of Scotland, the people, and their pride in the nation. Having been banned for many years as dangerous, possibly due to the 1746 Proscription Act, the Scots today hold fiercely to their restored symbol. They still carry them into battle (they did so in WWII, to their regiment-mates' chagrin) and refuse to forsake them.

There are different types of bagpipes, but most people are familiar with the Great Highland Bagpipes (*Pìob Mhòr*), and indeed, the sound from a properly played pipe is impressive and moving. While it was developed in Scotland, there are bagpipe traditions in many parts of the Celtic world, including Ireland, northern Spain (Galicia), and Wales.

The earliest bagpipe references are from the 15th century, but they could have been used as early as the 6th century. They were used for formal ceremonies, military marches, and were often used in hereditary clans such as the MacArthurs, MacDonalds, Mackays, and the MacCrimmons.

The music from the bagpipes was originally called *Piobaireachd*, which means "piping" in Gaelic. It has also been called *ceòl mòr*, or "great music." Other music, such as Strathspeys, reels, jigs, and hornpipes, became popular later as examples of "light music."

Harp and Fiddle

Stringed instruments have been known in Scotland since at least the Iron Age. Lyres were found on the Isle of Skye dating from 2,300 BCE, Europe's oldest surviving stringed instrument. The Scottish *clàrsach*, or harp, was pretty much regarded as the national instrument. However, it was displaced by the bagpipes sometime around the 15th century. Stone carvings indicate that the harp was known by and used by the Picts, perhaps even before the 9th century. An oral tradition meant that poets and storytellers were highly respected, as they were holders of genealogies, histories, and legends.

They were honored at all levels, and to kill a bard was a grievous sin. They were usually the highest advisor to the king, and often worked as historians, genealogists, and experts on the Brehon Law, as well. Brehon Law was a complex system of legal rules that permeated Celtic culture.

Some modern harp players include Savourna Stevenson, Maggie MacInnes, and the band, Sìleas. A CD from Sìleas (*Beating Harps*) was one of my first purchases of Celtic music, and I was instantly hooked.

Scottish traditional fiddling has many regional styles, including the upbeat styles of the northern isles, and the slow airs of the northeast. The instrument probably arrived in the 17th century from mainland Europe and has become an integral part of the Scottish music tradition. Scottish and Irish fiddling was the precursor to the Appalachian fiddling in the United States and has also been "parent" to the fiddling of Cape Breton in Nova Scotia. Musicians such as Natalie McMaster have brought this style to the worldwide stage. I saw Natalie McMaster at a Dublin Irish Festival where she brought her five children on stage to fiddle and dance.

Accordion

Thanks mostly to the work of Phil Cunningham, whose piano accordion was an essential ingredient in Silly Wizard, many artists have begun to use this instrument in both folk and rock music in Scotland. The melodeon was popular in the early 20th century, especially among country folk, and was considered part of the bothy band tradition. Bothy bands came from the farming culture of 19th century Scotland, from the small communities that formed in clusters of cottages.

Tin Whistle

While usually associated with Ireland, Scotland also has a tradition of the tin whistle, and has been found with pottery dating as far back as the 14th and 15th centuries. It is common for pipers and flute players to also play the tin whistle. A single tin whistle, well-played, can be the most haunting and wistful sound one has heard.

Fionnphort

The Dancing

The Piping tradition is strongly tied to both the traditional step-dance of the Highlands and the singing, much of which mimics the sounds of the bagpipes. Highland balls are still rather more frequent than you might expect, and of course weddings and other celebrations are everywhere. A *cèilidh* (country dance or party) is common, especially in the smaller villages.

There are group dances, like line and square dancing that's popular in America. Indeed, this is likely where it originated, with Highlanders having emigrated to areas such as Virginia and South Carolina in the mid-18th century. Typically, there will be a fiddler, perhaps some other instruments, and, rather than a caller, there is a set sequence of moves to any given tune. These dances include line promenades, corners, weaving in and out, all like square dancing.

A traditional form of Scottish dancing is the Highland Fling, or the Sword Dance. Typically, if you've been to any sort of Highland Games, you will have seen flocks of pre-teen girls in pastel-colored checkered stockings and skirts, one arm on their hip and another in the air, hopping about on one foot and then the other in a set pattern. Traditionally, there are two swords on the ground, in a crossed pattern. This dance was traditionally done before a battle, and usually by a man, if the dancer could complete the steps without stepping on a sword, they would be victorious.

The Quiraing, Isle of Skye

The Songs

Vocal music is very traditional to Scotland, especially the ballads and laments, sung by a lone singer, with or without accompaniment. There is a tradition of *puirt à beulè*, or "mouth music," traditionally sung solo without instruments, and consists of rhymes in a set pattern, perhaps originally for helping the rhythm during the work of mashing the barley, or waulking the wool, cleaning the wool. These are also called bothy songs, as men working together on farms lived in a bothy, cottage. Julie Fowlis does some lovely puirt à beul songs, as does Sìleas.

Now that you understand a little of the history behind the music, you will want to sing along with some of these rousing jigs and sad ballads at the pub, right? Don't feel shy; people do it all the time.

Sad songs. *Bidh Clann Ulaidh; Beloved Gregor; Green Grow the Rushes Oh; Thomas the Rhymer; The Cruel Mother; Tam Lin; Amazing Grace; Auld Lang Syne; Ca' the Yowes; Caledonia.*

Happy songs (or at least enthusiastic). *Donald Where's Yer Troosers?; Mhàiri's Wedding; Nancy Whisky; Hame Drunk Cam I; Jock Stewart; Blue Blazing Blind Drunk* (do you sense a theme here?).

Rebel songs. *The Flowers of the Forest; The Campbells are Coming; Hieland Laddie; Johnnie Cope; Killiecrankie; Ye Jacobites by Name; A Song to the Prince; The Skye Boat Song; Will Ye No Come Back Again?; Both Sides of the Tweed; Wha'll be King but Charlie; Wi' a Hundred Pipers; Charlie is my Darling; The Highland Widow's Lament; Arthur McBride.*

Love songs. *The Queen of Argyll; My Love is Like a Red; Red Rose; Wild Mountain Thyme; The Bleacher Lassie o' Kelvinhaugh; The Road and the Miles to Dundee; The Bonnie Banks of Loch Lomond; The Banks o' Red Roses.*

Bothy songs. *The Rovin' Ploughboy; MacPherson's Rant; The Bonny Ship the Diamond; The Gypsy Laddies; Johnnie O'Breadislie.*

Some are simply tunes, rather than songs. *Lament for the Children; Black-haired Lad; A Piper's Warning to his Master; A Cholla mo Rùn; MacCrimmon's Sweetheart; Cradle Song.*

Eilan Donan Castle

Of course, on any typical pub night, you may hear many Irish and American songs sprinkled in with Scottish favorites. Just because the tune is from another land, doesn't mean people don't like it! I've often heard *Country Roads* (West Virginia), *Daydream Believer*, and *Piano Man* at pub sings.

Finding the Music

"A Scot of poetic temperament, and without religious exultation, drops as if by nature into the public house; but what else is a man to do in this dog's weather."
-Robert Louis Stevenson

Pubs are the community living room in Scotland. It's a place where people gather to relax, socialize, and talk about their day. Perhaps they complain about the weather, share some funny stories, toast a pint, and listen to some music. You can find them in every size and description across the country. Do keep in mind that not all have music, not all served food (food service usually stops around 8pm or 9pm), and none allow smoking (since 2006) inside. Sometimes there is an outdoor "beer garden" to accommodate those who must light up.

Children can be welcome in the early evenings, and sometimes well-behaved dogs as well in some establishments. While you must be eighteen to purchase alcohol, children as young as fourteen are welcome if the pub has a children's license, as long as they don't drink alcohol! That child must be accompanied by an adult, and may be restricted to certain areas, such as the restaurant area of the pub. Once the food is no longer served, however, the children are no longer allowed in the area.

Pubs, especially in the less populated areas, might not be open during mid- afternoon hours, say between 2pm and 5pm. Some may close for the winter season. If you are in a strongly Protestant area, such as the "Wee Free" islands in the Outer Hebrides, they may be closed all day on Sunday. Do some research before your trip so you aren't disappointed. This isn't based on law, but custom, so your mileage may vary.

Perhaps finding a pub with music isn't quite as easy in Scotland as it is in Ireland, but it's still not difficult if you're in the countryside rather than a city.

There are several website resources I've listed in the Appendix that might help you find the perfect pub for some lovely Scottish music, including that of the Traditional Music & Song Association of Scotland. They have a list of local folk festivals as well as the pub "sessions."

A session could mean a solo performer, a group of twenty taking turns or playing together, or anything in between. These are not usually professional performers, but locals who just love playing, and often tourists joining in. Their performances are not polished, but they are genuine in a way that set shows are not.

If you bring your own instrument and/or your voice, you will be welcome to join. Music likely won't start until around 9 or 10pm each night, but do get there earlier, as space is at a premium. We prefer to find B&Bs that are within staggering distance of a pub with music, so there are no worries of drinking and driving.

Most advertised "traditional Scottish nights" in the bigger hotels are staged performances, with dancers and singers with honed skills. They may be slick professional performers, but they're still fun.

Some of the places in Edinburgh known for good traditional music include Sandy Bell's, Royal Oak Bar, and the Wee Folk Club.

Duart Castle

Literature, Shows and Movies

Many books, television shows, and movies have made their home in Scotland. Not only those based on the rich history of the land, but those with some fantasy or literary license. I've listed a few of them below, with a list of places where you can visit scenes from the work. While the scope of this book is not large enough to make an exhaustive list, I've listed some of my favorites.

Movies

- **Brave.** While *Brave* is an animated film, much of the animation was based on real locations in Scotland, such as the Calanais standing stones on the Isle of Lewis. Dunnottar Castle and Glen Affric provided inspiration for the animators as well.
- **Braveheart.** Various historic locations, such as Stirling and Edinburgh, are portrayed in the film. While some footage includes Glen Nevis, Glen Coe, Loch Neven, and Fort William, much of the movie was filmed in Ireland due to weather difficulties in Scotland.
- **The Da Vinci Code.** Bringing Rosslyn Chapel into the limelight, this thriller has played an important part in a resurgence of interest in this exquisite chapel.
- **Chariots of Fire.** If you walk the West Sands Beach in St. Andrews, you will walk in the footsteps of the actors in this Oscar-winning film. Edinburgh and Sma' Glen were also used as locations.
- **Entrapment:** Duart Castle is the home of the MacLean Clan and located on the Isle of Mull. It was used in this film with Sean Connery and Catherine Zeta-Jones. Eilean Donan Castle was also used for some shots.
- **Harry Potter.** Most people will be familiar with the Glenfinnan Aqueduct due to the many panning shots of the Hogwarts Express shooting across the scenic place. The castle itself is constructed of several other castles, with added animations. Glen Coe, Loch Shiel, Loch Eilt, and Loch Morar are also used as filming locations.
- **Highlander.** This film (and the subsequent television series and sequels) used many parts of the highlands in filming. Eilan Donan Castle is the most recognizable location used on the set of the original movie, starring Christopher Lambert and Sean Connery. Other parts of the film were shot in Skye, Loch Shiel and Glen Coe.

- **Local Hero.** This feel-good film was mostly filmed in Pennan, Aberdeenshire and on Camusdarach Beach, in Morar. Banff and Loch Tarff also played host to the movie sets.
- **Monty Python and the Holy Grail.** Most of the castle scenes in this comedy were filmed at Doune Castle, except near the end. Castle Stalker was used for Castle of Aaaargh! Rannoch Moor and Glen Coe were also used, as well as Arnhall Castle, Sheriffmuir, Loch Tay and the Duke's Pass.
- **Rob Roy.** This film starring Liam Neeson was historically set in Balquhidder. The film, however, used Megginch Castle, Crichton Castle, Glen Coe, Glen Nevis, Rannoch Moor and Glen Tarbet.
- **Skyfall.** James Bond fans will remember the last part of the film, where they search for a place out of reach of all technology and end up in Scotland. The area this part was filmed in is known as Buachaille Etive Mor, near Glen Coe, and is noted for its stark beauty and desolation. Another James Bond film, *The World is Not Enough*, used Eilean Donan Castle as well.
- **Trainspotting.** This cult classic is mostly filmed in Glasgow, though the story was set in Edinburgh. Some filming was done on Rannoch Moor, near Glen Coe.
- **The Wicker Man.** A cult film from the 1970s, the towns of Gatehouse of Fleet, Newton Stewart, Creetown and Kirkcudbright were used for filming, in the Dumfries & Galloway regions. Plockton, St. Ninian's Cave and Culzean Castle in Ayrshire was also used for some of the film.

Television Series

- **Hamish Macbeth.** The town of Lochdubh is fictitious, but it was filmed in Plockton, Kyle of Lochalsh and the surrounding area. It stars Robert Carlyle as a rather peevish lone police officer in a small highland town. The setting of the town itself is stunning.
- **Monarch of the Glen.** The scenery in this show has been described as one of the main characters. Set in fictional Glenbogle, the filming was done at Ardverikie Estate, a massive turreted manor house in the highlands. While the house is not open to the public, private tours can sometimes be arranged, and the gatehouse (also

in the show) is available to rent as a self-catering property. Laggan is the town that is used, and Kingussie, Carrbridge and Broomhill Station make appearances. The River Pattack is used for many scenes.

- **Outlander, by Diana Gabaldon.** These books are mostly set in Scotland and have many locations both in the books and the television series filming. Castle Leod, home of the Clan McKenzie becomes Castle Leoch in the show (filmed at Castle Doune). Clava Cairns stone circle was the basis for Craig na Dun. Other locations in the books include Edinburgh Castle, Culloden Field, and Inverness. The filming locations include Falkland Palace, Blackness Castle, Midhope Castle and Culross Palace and Abbey.

- **Rebus.** Based on Ian Rankin's Inspector Rebus novels. The series aired with two seasons starring John Hannah, but after a hiatus, Ken Stott took over as Inspector Rebus for two more seasons. Set in and around Edinburgh, these seasons were typically two-hour episodes within a four-episode season, also known as mini- series. What makes these mini-series different from the typical mini-series is they ran over four seasons, rather than just one season as typical for these types of programs.

- **Taggart.** A police procedural program based in Strathclyde, a suburb of Glasgow. This has been a long running series which began in 1983, starring Mark McManus as DCI Jim Taggart until his death in 1994. The series ran until 2010 under the same name, though there was no longer was a DCI Taggart in the program.

Books/Authors

- **Iain Banks.** Banks, who died in 2013, was a Scottish author whose books have been adapted in theater, radio, and television, and he has been honored many times by the Science Fiction and mainstream writing communities. He was born in Dunfermline, Fife, and set many of his books in Edinburgh.

- **Tony Black.** Edinburgh-based crime writer. Popular for the Gus Drury series. He was an award-winning journalist, with works appearing in many UK papers and periodicals. Since turning his hand to fiction, he's become one of Edinburgh's most revered crime writers of the 21st century, earning him fans such as Ian Rankin (Inspector Rebus series) and Irvine Welsh (Trainspotting).

- **Robert Burns.** Burns is known as The Bard in Scotland and lived in the 18th century. He is celebrated worldwide and regarded as Scotland's National Poet. He lived near the town of Ayr in Ayrshire, and the house he lived in is now the Burns Cottage Museum. He also lived in Tarbolton, Mauchline, Dumfries and Edinburgh.
- **Dorothy Dunnett.** Best known for her historical fiction series The Lymond Chronicles, Dunnett lived in Edinburgh. Her novels took place mostly along the borders of Scotland but ranged widely across the world.
- **Diana Gabaldon.** Outlander novels, see the entry in the Television Series section above.
- **Neil Gunn.** Born in Dunbeath, Caithness, Gunn moved south to Kirkcudbrightshire. His novels and stories were influential with many modern writers.
- **Compton Mackenzie.** Best known for his novels *Whisky Galore* set in the Hebrides and *Monarch of the Glen* set in the Scottish Highlands, Mackenzie was born in England, but remained fiercely proud of his Scottish ancestry.
- **Karen Marie Moning.** Moning has several historical fiction novels set during the more evocative of times throughout Scottish history, novelizing famous events such as the Glencoe massacre, among others.
- **Ian Rankin.** Rankin hails from Fife, but his Inspector Rebus series is mostly set in Edinburgh, where he now lives.
- **Kate Robbins.** Author of the Highland Chief series, Robbins has some steamy romances set in the Highlands of Scotland.
- **J. K. Rowling.** Harry Potter novels, see the entry in the Movies section above.
- **Sir Walter Scott.** Timeless classics such as *Ivanhoe* and *Rob Roy* are part of the rich heritage Sir Walter Scott leaves for the world. He was born near the Grassmarket in Edinburgh, though lived in the Borders for a time. Many of his novels are thus set in the city, or in the romantic highlands. *Waverly*, for instance, was set in the Highlands as a tale of the Jacobite Rising of 1745.

- **Robert Louis Stevenson.** The author of *Kidnapped*, *Treasure Island*, and *Strange Case of Dr. Jekyll and Mr. Hyde* should need no introduction. His novels have been inspiration for generations of novelists and storytellers. He was born and lived in Edinburgh, though he traveled in search of health many times.
- **Nigel Tranter.** While he began as a writer about the history of castles, Tranter explores characters in his Bruce Trilogy, MacGregor Trilogy and Master of Gray Trilogy.

Isle of Lewis

STUNNING SHOTS

How better to capture the moment, the memory, the mood, than to take a photograph of the stunning vista you see before you on your trip to Scotland? One of the exquisite draws of this island to millions of tourists are the beautiful sights which are everywhere, and it takes very little time (if any) to travel from one stunning landscape to the next. It's all contained in a compact, green package, ready to share with your envious loved ones.

Edinburgh Castle

Photographs provide a great service to both the photographer, and his friends and family. They record the memory to share and to relive later.

There are many times I've looked back on my photos and remembered a scene I had forgotten, relived a memory I had lost. This is also a reason I write my trip reports in such detail, I know my own memory is rather faulty, so I jot down notes every time I sit down to eat during the trip. This helps me write down the narrative later and keeps my memory strong years afterwards. It also helps me realize where I took some of the photographs.

The Preparation

While there may be a few out there still using film, most people take digital photographs now, and most of those use their phone rather than a camera. If you are still on film, then some of this advice must be adjusted for this fact, so keep this in mind. However, one of the biggest advantages of digital photography is the ability to take as many photographs as you have memory space for, and sort later the ones you wish to spend money on printing. A decent digital camera before you leave deserves a bit of research. I'm not much of a movie-taker, but some people prefer video to photographs. If so, much of this will also apply to the video recorder shopping.

The Equipment

Not everyone needs or wants a professional grade camera. These can cost over $5,000, and most people don't have this in the budget. Even high-grade amateur cameras, which usually run between $400 and $1,000, are outside most people's budget and desire. However, a decent amateur camera can be gotten for about $150-$200, and, in my opinion, are well worth the investment. You should, however, do your research, and decide which camera is right for you. If you are not planning on printing your photographs in huge sizes for hanging on the wall, your smartphone camera should be sufficient.

There is an excellent site at Digital Photography Review which allows you to choose cameras by feature and compare them side by side. I have used it many times to choose my next piece of equipment. You will need to decide which features are important to you. Since I take a lot of landscape shots, and often from the window of a moving car, long optical zoom and fast shutter speed are very important to me. The ability to shoot in RAW format (which doesn't let the camera do any editing of the image) is also important to me, as I do a lot of post-production manipulation in Photoshop. Is low light photography important to you, for night shots or party shots? How about close ups for flowers and other macro photography? Once you know what is important, you are ready to choose a decent camera.

By the way, some of the best shots I've taken have been from a point-and-shoot $80 camera. Good equipment is helpful but is NOT essential. The art is truly in the eye of the artist, not the equipment they use.

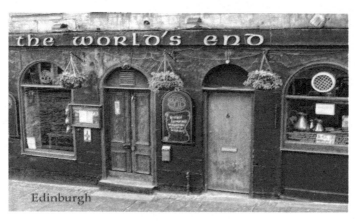

Edinburgh

The Accessories

Many cameras come with interchangeable lenses, one for macro, one for zoom, etc. The higher-end professional cameras have this as a matter of course. The point-and-shoots do not, for the most part. The rest of us are in the middle. My camera of choice right now is the Nikon CoolPix P900, which does NOT have a removable lens. The installed lens can zoom 83X and can do a decent macro shot. I'm happy with this range and would rather not mess with multiple lenses. This is my personal choice, and it may not be yours, so experiment with a few. Go to the store, pick up the camera with all its accessories. Do you want to be hiking up a mountain and through an airport, carrying all this? Or is it worth it to you?

Memory, memory, memory, without it, you are done with your digital diary. Uploading to the cloud might not always be practical. There are several options to make sure you have enough on your trip. Memory sticks of any type are pretty cheap.

North Coast

My option this last trip was simply to take enough sticks to make sure I never ran out of room. I never came close, even after 9,900 photos. I always, always, however, take at least one more than I think I will need in case one gets corrupted or lost. Another option I've done in the past is take a laptop and download the card each night. This is fine if you are already planning on taking a laptop, not so much if you'd rather not carry the extra weight.

It's worth a note to say if you do, for some reason, accidentally erase the photos from your card, don't despair. Also, don't touch it. Don't try to take more pictures on that card and save it until you can get in touch with an expert. The expert should be able to get most of the data from it.

My friend Carla did this on our trip to Scotland; 1,200 photos erased in the blink of an eye. She kept it without taking more photos on that card, and when she returned, she was able to get back about 90% of those precious memories she captured with the help of a data recovery specialist.

Hoy

The Method

Scotland is truly a land of wonders. It is not a large place, but it is packed with stunning seascapes, sandy beaches, rocky forts, romantic ruins, and bucolic pastures.

When I went to Scotland in June of 2008, in twenty-three days, I had racked up over five thousand photos. I believe in the theory you take as many photos as you possibly can on-site, as you can always sift through them later. Different perspectives, different lighting, and different levels, a couple will turn out well.

You can't as easily go back and revisit the site. Even the few times I have revisited a place and took a photograph, I've discovered the landscape has changed. Traveling to the Isle of Skye in 2000, and then again in

2008, parts of it looked completely different due to construction, time, and weather.

In Scotland, you are tempted to stop every five minutes on your journey to take a photo of the lamb nursing by the side of the road, the ruins on the hill, the charming, thatched cottage on the road. Go ahead and do it! Do it safely, mind, there are usually small lay-bys (pullouts) which you can turn into for a very short period (don't park there, they are for passing, not parking), or driveways you can turn into. This is a country made for photo opportunities, after all! After you've seen your hundredth sheep or so, you may be less tempted to stop at the sight of each one.

You should keep in mind some basic photography truths, but also keep in mind these are rules, and rules are sometimes meant to be broken.

- **The rule of thirds.** Composition is more interesting when objects and horizon lines are on the top or bottom third of the picture, or the left/right third.
- **Lines.** Roads, fences, and other lines lead the eye into a particular spot, make sure the spot has something interesting.
- **Scale.** The mountain photo is great, but how big is it? Take a shot with a flower, tree, or cottage in the foreground to lend a perspective of scale.
- **Weather.** The weather in Scotland is part of the landscape. Use it to your advantage! There's a storm coming in, wouldn't a dark cloud look dramatic over the castle? Move your body until you can get the shot lined up right. And then run for the car before the deluge hits!
- **Perspective.** More interesting points of view can change the feel of a photo. Shooting straight up on a castle wall or a tree, or down on a flower can work wonders.
- **Action.** A standing sheep is lovely, but getting a lamb while it nurses, or a pony while running makes the photo much more interesting.
- **Lighting.** Sunrise and sunset, storms and clouds, and the ever-present mists of Scotland can make some amazing atmospheric shots. One reason I like staying in one place for several days is to

have several opportunities to take photos at different times of the day and night.

The Locations

While all of Scotland is picturesque and charming, and different people like different things, there are certain places, subjects and areas which stand out as being incredibly photogenic.

- **Cliffs.** Scotland is rugged and rough in its landscape and has a long and varied coastline. My favorite place in the world is to be on a sea cliff, looking down at the ocean crashing upon the rocks far below me. I love the mix of sea, wind, and earth, and I feel like I'm standing on the edge of the earth. As a result, I take many of my photographs in such spots. Whether it is Kilt Rock on the Isle of Skye, or the fine sandy beach at Luskentyre on the Isle of Lewis, or the hexagonal rocks on the Isle of Staffa, I love the places where the water meets the land.
- **Water.** Lochs and rivers have coastlines as well, and Scotland certainly has its share of picturesque places along its waterways. The country is practically split in half by one! Many large lakes, such as Loch Lomond, Loch Tay, or the Lake of Mentieth have stunning scenery to capture.
- **Castles.** Scotland has hundreds of castles, ranging from grand palaces which will rent you a room for the night, to crumbling ruins which barely hold a full wall against the tide of time. Each

is unique and has photographic charm of its own. Some areas are more castle-rich than others, such as Aberdeen and its Castle Trail, but there are random ruins wherever you go. Some seemingly don't even have a name, it being lost in time. Today, they are just a nuisance to the local farmer who cannot farm this part of the land.

- **Critters.** Sheep, Highland cows, goats, donkeys, chickens, and horses. There are more, but these are what I see most of in Scotland. Sheep, and some more sheep. And look, there are some sheep! And a horse. And more sheep. If you visit in April or May, you will see adorable lambs running after their mothers, looking for lunch.

- **Cities.** Edinburgh is a jewel in the crown of the world, with beautiful architecture, but don't discount Glasgow. While it has had a reputation in the past for being the workaday poor cousin of Edinburgh, it has revamped itself into a city of culture and art. Inverness, in my opinion, is more a base to explore the Highlands, but it has its charms as well. Aberdeen is known as the Granite City, showing off many buildings that sparkle in the sun after the rain. There are throngs of people going about their merry day to photograph, and unique sites such as the commanding castles in Stirling and Edinburgh, and the People's Palace in Glasgow.

- **Flowers.** Scotland has many incredible gardens, ranging from the formal gardens in Glasgow to those in countryside castles, like Inverary or Dunvegan. Most cottages and houses have small, well-tended flower gardens in their homes, and the Scots take pride in these miniature beauties. Purple heather will dominate in autumn, while wildflowers are lovely among the green throughout the spring and summer.

- **Cottages.** Ah, the charming, thatched cottage. They transport you back to imagined romantic past lives, filled with peat smoke and traditional music. Many of these are becoming impractical, but the Scots realize their tourism draw, and preserve those which are left for the teeming tours of photographers. There are several folk villages that preserve these places of history, so you can see what it was like to live in such a place.

- **People.** The ever-friendly people of Scotland are usually game for posing for a photograph. Especially if they are red-haired with freckles or wearing a kilt, you won't be the first to ask them! Often, after a few pints in a pub, they'll not say no. Do be respectful, though, these folk are trying to go about their day, and some are quite busy with their lives.

- **Stones.** Yes, stones! Scotland is a very rocky country. And while the cliffs are made of stone, so are the Neolithic burial sites, the stone circles, the ogham memorials, the Pictish towers, and the Celtic crosses. There is great texture and pattern in stones of all types. The north has many of these, but they dot the entire land.

Isle of Mull

- **Churches.** Scotland has a strange dichotomy in religion, with the Catholic Highlanders and the Wee Free islands, but there are still lovely churches to both belief systems around the country. Larger communities may have temples or churches of other faiths, such as Muslim, Jewish, Methodist, and others. Many abbeys stand in ruins since medieval times. Either way, they are an important part of the cultural and physical landscape of the land.

- **Kilts,** OK, so I have a soft spot for men in kilts, and Scotland is one of the few places where you can see men dressed in them, randomly on the street. Not part of a Renaissance Festival, Scottish Festival, or part of a play, just normal everyday men walking to work, to church, to school. It's not everywhere, mind you, but it is often enough that you will see it fairly frequently, especially if you get up higher into the North Highlands.

A note about pests! Some of the best shots will be early morning and late afternoon, due to the incredible light. However, Scotland only has a few mosquitoes, which most people are well familiar with. Much more annoying are the swarms of biting midges. Midges are tiny, biting flies, smaller than gnats. This means they get through most mosquito netting, and they fly in swarms. They are most prevalent in the Highlands and Isles, and during dawn and dusk. I've used Skin So Soft to good effect in repelling them. Wind also helps, but it's more difficult to command the weather gods!

Dunrobin Castle Gardens

Whatever you do, do NOT be afraid of walking off the beaten path. Climb into the forest, up a rock, into a graveyard, around a stone wall, the possibilities are endless.

Of course, be aware of your surroundings and dress appropriately for your adventures. Bring what supplies are required, such as walking sticks, sturdy shoes, water, and food, etc. If you are truly adventurous, go on a mountain walk (please, with an experienced guide). Keep in mind some sites, such as the Tomb of the Eagles, are only accessible if you walk THROUGH someone's yard or field. This is allowed but do be respectful with the owners' permission (as this may be a working farm or other place of business) and do no harm to the property.

Skye Blackhouse

The Aftermath

Inevitably, you get home and look at your photos, and you are disappointed. You remember it being much more breathtaking than the photo could capture. This is, unfortunately, due to the limitations of modern technology. While today's cameras are incredible, they still are not the human eye, and can only capture a thin slice of the wonder we see with our own incredibly complex eye structure. Even the eye cannot truly see all our mind imagines when we look upon a fantasy landscape like Scotland. Our imagination fills the faery hills and standing stones with mystery and wonder. Our eye only sees part of this, and the camera captures even less of it.

One of the reasons I manipulate my photographs is I want to share what my mind saw at the location, not what my eye saw, or what the camera captured. I want to share this with those who couldn't be there to experience it with me. It's a tall order and sometimes very difficult to accomplish, but I work at it until I am mostly satisfied with my results.

I usually print my photos in small format first, to see how they come out in that format (the computer screen sometimes isn't the best portrayal of print photograph). I then order the prints larger to sell. I use a company called White House Custom Copies. You can upload your photos to their server and receive them a couple days later. I've never had a problem with WHCC, and their customer service is top notch. I've also printed canvas prints with Simply Canvas, and books and calendars at Lulu. There are many ways to share your memories with those you love!

Bunressan

HAGGIS AND CULLENSKINK

Like their "downstairs neighbor," Scotland has long had a reputation for boring and tasteless food. However, once they realized that they had a wealth of natural game, produce and spices, and stopped exporting all the yummy stuff to England, Scotland experienced a renaissance in cuisine and now take great pride in it. Perhaps having had the Auld Alliance with France helped, and the Scots have begun to send their chefs to France to learn the techniques. They come back and use the fantastic local ingredients, with wonderful results.

Now, you will still get street food and take-away places, but the high-end restaurants will not leave you wanting. Takeaway is a great way to experience fantastic ethnic food. Some of the best Indian food I've ever had was at Scottish take-away joints in Orkney and Lewis, and a fantastic sit-down Indian restaurant in Edinburgh.

Breakfasts

If you are staying at Bed & Breakfasts (B&Bs), you will be served a fantastic breakfast by your hosts. One option is almost always the Full Scottish Breakfast, also known as the *All-Day Breakfast*:

- This starts off with an egg (usually fried, but it can often be poached or scrambled by choice).
- Then a bit of fried or grilled bacon is added. This is not like American bacon, it's more like a slice of fatty ham, much thicker than ours, almost a fattier version of Canadian Bacon. They call our type of bacon "streaky bacon."

- Add a couple of link sausage, these are usually not very spicy or peppery.
- Black pudding, a slice of sausage made with grains, spices, and pigs' blood.
- White pudding, like the black pudding, but without the blood, and made with different spices.
- Grilled half tomato.
- Grilled mushrooms.
- Baked beans.
- Fried bread (sliced white bread fried in the flavored oil used to prepare the rest of the breakfast).
- Haggis, Try it! It is the national dish, Haggis is a spicy, grain-filled sausage, traditionally made with sheep offal and cooked in a sheep's stomach. While modern commercial versions use higher quality meats, traditionally handmade haggis should definitely be experienced. It is, if done right, very tasty and moist. Robert Burns even wrote "Address to a Haggis," which is trotted out and performed at Robert Burns suppers each year:

Fair fa' your honest, sonsie face, Great Chieftain o' the Puddin-race! Aboon them a' ye tak your place, Painch, tripe, or thairm:
Weel are ye wordy of a grace
As lang's my arm

Other options may include smoked salmon with scrambled eggs, porridge (aka oatmeal), various cold cereals, fresh and stewed/canned fruit, poached eggs. In addition, there is coffee, tea, milk, and often several types of juice available. Sometimes there are homemade jams and jellies, scones, or pancakes as well. Occasionally, I've had muesli, or a mixed fruit/grain/cream concoction that was delicious.

Now you know why the Full Scottish Breakfast is also called the All-Day Breakfast. You will NOT go away hungry from a Scottish breakfast, and most likely, you won't be hungry again until 2 or 3pm, at which point, most places will no longer be serving lunch. So, eat less and have a normal lunchtime, or be prepared with snacks to keep you until dinner.

Food

Western civilization is extremely food oriented. We meet for lunch and we meet for drinks. If we have someone over as a guest, we offer them a drink, and we sit down for a dinner party. Barbecues and picnics are how families meet up. We obsess about our weight, our presentation, the taste, style, and healthiness of food, everything associated with the act of eating. So how do the Scottish do all of this?

My restaurant of choice in Scotland (or anywhere else in Great Britain or Ireland) is the pub. Sometimes this is because it's the only thing open at 2 or 3pm serving food by the time I've worked off the huge Scottish Breakfast. Also, the food is inexpensive, and Gastropubs have raised the bar on quality food.

Seafood Platter at Three Chimneys

Traditionally, pubs have been primarily for drinking, with a packet of crisps (potato chips), pork scratching (pork rinds), or peanuts as an afterthought. Some pubs served "pies and a pint," the pies being meat and potatoes encased in pastry and baked and held in the hand to eat. Now, traditional pub grub can include those same meat pies, plus hearty stews, fish-and-chips, carvery roasts, and whatever the pub's chef can conjure up on the day. A Ploughman's Lunch (bits of cheese, relish or pickle, leftover carved roast from the previous day, and some bread) is a holdover from this time. While many pubs have their own signature meals on their menu, there are certain dishes you will usually always find at almost any pub worth its salt in Scotland.

- **Fish-n-chips.** Originally brought to the British Isles by Italian immigrants, this dish has become synonymous with England, Wales, Ireland, and Scotland. Flaky white fish (usually cod or whiting) is battered and deep fried and served thick-cut chips (fries).
- **Mussels.** Especially in the coastal areas, mussels are a staple, most often served in a white wine and garlic sauce, and a side of traditional brown bread and butter.
- **Steak & ale pie.** A thick, dark savory type of stew loaded with chunks of beef, potato, carrot baked in a flaky pastry, I've also seen it with lamb, known as lamb and ale pie.
- **Deep fried mushrooms.** Coated in batter or crumbs, and deep fried. Often with aioli sauce/garlic mayo.
- **Goat's cheese salad.** Sometimes the cheese is coated in crumbs then fried, sometimes baked, sometimes cold. Usually served on salad greens with a sweet chutney of some sort, like cranberry compote.
- **Soups.** Unless it's a "stew," it will likely be pureed. Vegetable soup, potato soup, mushroom soup, unless the menu lists "clear soup," you are more than likely to be served a creamy puree, so be aware. Adding to the creaminess, almost always, fresh cream is also added, either in the blending process or by spoon at the end (you'll see swirls of white in the soup).
- **Shepherd's Pie.** Savory minced/ground lamb and vegetables topped with mashed potatoes and baked until the potatoes are golden. Cottage Pie is most often offered in tourist establishments. This is the same as Shepherd's Pie but is made with beef rather than lamb.
- **Burgers.** Yes, lots of burgers. Those served in upscale eateries are made with high-quality beef and lots of topping choices. Take-aways also offer burgers on their menu, which are highly processed. Chicken sandwiches are becoming very popular.
- **Scallops.** The Scottish love their scallops, and they are delicious! Occasionally I've gotten them with the roe still attached.
- **Smoked salmon.** This dish is often served with traditional brown bread and butter, perhaps some capers or dill dressing.

- **Scotch eggs.** Hard-boiled eggs deep fried in a crust of sausage and breadcrumbs. If done right, it's delicious!
- **Curry & chips.** Try it! I was skeptical at first, but curry makes an excellent sauce for your chips.
- **Prawn cocktail with Marie Rose sauce.** Unlike the tomatoey sauce in America, Marie Rose sauce is made from mayonnaise and ketchup, sometimes with a little Worcestershire Sauce. Small prawns are added to the sauce and mixed well, then served on a bed of lettuce or in a small bowl.
- **Bangers & Mash.** Sausage and mashed potatoes; what can be better?
- **Toad in the Hole.** A sausage baked in a Yorkshire pudding, covered in gravy.
- **Sticky toffee pudding.** A steamed sponge cake made with chopped dates, covered in a butter rum toffee sauce, usually served warm.
- *Cranachan.* A traditional dessert with raspberries, toasted oats, cream, honey, and whisky.
- **Bread and butter pudding**. Traditional bread pudding, made with chunks of stale bread in an eggy-custardy mix with cinnamon or all spice, most often with raisins, and served with a whisky sauce, and warm pouring custard on the side.
- **Bannoffee Pie.** As the name implies, this is banana and toffee made into a creamy pie. Onto a cookie crumb base, fresh sliced bananas are layered, then the creamy banana-toffee cream is poured on and refrigerated until set. It's served with generous lashings of fresh whipped cream and drizzles of toffee sauce on top, and chocolate shavings, and sometimes chopped fresh nuts.

Hamish the Hieland Coo

Some pubs have different items, of course, and the fancier they want to look, the more haute they try to make their cuisine. I've seen a couple failed efforts here and there, but for the most part, the Gastropubs (and even those regular pubs that care) do a pretty good job firing up the food.

If you would rather not eat at the pub, the "normal" restaurants are great, as well. I'm a big fan of seafood, and Scotland has wonderful dishes made with salmon, prawns, mackerel, mussels, scallops, oysters, and anything else you can imagine. Scottish beef is top-notch, but I usually go for the lamb, as it is more difficult to find in the US, and it is everywhere on the menu in Scotland. Their ethnic restaurants tend to be delicious as well, some of the best Indian and Chinese food I've had has been in Ireland and Scotland.

Street food is also an option, I've had pancakes (crepes), fish-n-chips, chips and curry, and gyros served roadside in mobile food vans. Or you can get supplies at the grocery store and snack on the road. If you are staying in a self-catering place, you will have a full kitchen to make your own creations.

Here are some other traditional treats you might find and try:

- **Angus Beef.** Scotland is world-famous for its high-quality Aberdeen Angus beef, and most pubs will serve it as steaks and as burgers and are proud of saying so.
- **Arbroath Smokies.** These are a flavorful sausage made using traditional methods dating back to the 1880s.
- **Bannocks.** A type of quick bread. It varies in size slightly, from about the same thickness as a scone, to a sort of a flat griddle cake. They were useful for a quick snack out on the moors and stayed fresh all day.
- **Cock-a-leekie soup.** As the name implies, this is chicken and leek soup. The traditional method of making this soup would have also included slices of prunes in the broth.
- **Cullen Skink.** A thick Scottish chowder made with smoked haddock, potatoes, and onions. Keep in mind this is smoked fish, so it has a nice, strong taste!

- **Deep fried Mars Bar.** The Scots will deep fry anything, haggis, slices of pizza, and the Mars Bar. Frozen candy bars are battered and then deep fried, and often served with ice cream in some shops! Try it if you dare!
- **Drop Scones.** Similar to American pancakes, these are usually made sweet, with bits of date, raisins (sultanas) or other fruit inside. I've occasionally seen cheese scones as well.
- **Edinburgh Rock.** This is a rock candy sold on the streets of Edinburgh. Mind your teeth!
- **Finnan Haddies.** A smoked haddock that originated in the Aberdeen fishing village of Findon.
- **Forfar Bridie.** A small meat pastry or pie, like a Welsh pasty. Meat and vegetables are placed on one side of a round pastry which is then folded in half, edges pinched closed, then baked until done.
- **Red Grouse.** A typical Highland game bird on many menus. August 12th is the start of the hunting season, so if you are in Scotland on The Glorious Twelfth, watch for it!
- **Highland Oatcakes.** These thick, tasty oatcakes are similar to thick crackers and are a great base to serve with a bit of butter, honey, or jam spread on them.
- **Loch Fyne Kippers.** Kippers are sort of like larger sardines, not as salty, and often served warm with breakfast.
- **Neeps and tatties.** The traditional name for rutabaga (turnips) and potatoes, usually a mixed mashup of the two, with some spices and cream folded in.
- **Porridge.** Oatmeal served often for breakfast, sometimes with cream, butter, or sultanas.
- **Tablet.** Essentially, this is a firmer type of Scottish fudge which has a much higher sugar content than American fudge.
- **Scotch Pie.** A double-crusted, meat and vegetable filled pie. Similar to English pork pies.
- **Seaweed.** Several different sorts of seaweed are added to cheese, salads and other treats on Scottish menus.
- **Shortbread.** Scotland is famous for its shortbread, and you can find tins of it for sale everywhere, from gift shops to the supermarket,

and even in petrol stations in their convenience store. The tins are famous for their romanticized Highlander images on the lid.

Some of the places we had some fantastic meals in Scotland included take- aways, ethnic restaurants, pubs, and higher-end places. One such place was Khushi's, an Indian restaurant in Edinburgh. This is a full-service Indian Restaurant with wonderful garlic naan and lamb sag. A note of caution, though, if you are tempted to try Irn Bru (see below under drinks), don't try it after eating garlic naan. This is not a favorable taste combination!

Indian restaurants are very popular in both England and Scotland, as England ruled over India for many years. During that time, many Indians emigrated to the British Isles, and made lives there. They brought their spices and palates to awaken local sensibilities to the wonders of Indian food.

Moving farther north, Craig's Bar in Grantown-on-Spey is great for an evening of pints and pies. They have lovely pies! Such options, Minty Lamb pie, Smokey Jo pie (potatoes, spinach, cream, and mushrooms), Chicken of Aragon pie, or the Heidi pie (goats' cheese, sweet potato, spinach, garlic, and onion). They also have dozens of whiskies to try. They take several and list descriptions on the blackboard each night, so you can decide if you want to try a peaty, oaky, or salty whisky that evening. Or all three! The owners are true characters; Robbie, and his mother, who was about to head to China for the Olympics on her own, staying in youth hostels.

Farther north, if you are near Inverness, drive down the A82 towards Loch Ness.

In possibly the only case in Scotland where there is a sign BEFORE the establishment appears, look for the Oakwood Restaurant. This place is run by a Scottish man and his French wife, she cooks, he makes wonderful rustic picnic tables. We had chicken breast stuffed with haggis in a blackcurrant reduction and deer meat goulash. Cranachan and whisky/honey crème brûlée for dessert!

If you make it up to Orkney, and need some great food late at night, try *Dil Se*, the Indian restaurant near the library. Their biryani is fantastic, as is their roshni lamb.

On the Isle of Lewis, in the main town of Stornoway, there is an Indian restaurant called Balti House, just at the south end of the frontage road. The folks who run it grew up in Aberdeen, and it is odd hearing Hindi and then English in a Scottish accent, but the food was fantastic. I had the chili garlic lamb, and J had the chicken tikka curry. It was spicy, but not hot, lots of flavor, very tender.

Moving on to the Isle of Lewis, we had some great meals there, as well. In Stornoway, there is an Indian restaurant called Balti House, the folks that run it are Indian and speak Hindi and will then switch to English with an Aberdeen accent. The food is delicious, and the décor charming.

Stornoway

On the Isle of Skye there is a fantastic place, called the Three Chimneys Restaurant, which earned a Michelin Star in 2014. Yes, it is out in the middle of nowhere. Yes, it is expensive. However, it is worth it, even for my foodie husband. Our table was near the front window, we could look out at the bay during the meal. The wait staff was very attentive and helpful, and the food was simply superb. For starters, we had seafood bisque, fennel soup (bright green!), and roast pigeon. For the main meal, I had the roast lamb, which was lightly drizzled with a wonderfully savory/sweet sauce. Dessert was a simple melt-in-your-mouth lemon sorbet parfait.

The Selkirk Grace

Attributed to Robert Burns, this small poem said before meals was already well known before Burns' time, under other names. It is in Scots, traditionally, but I've provided both Scots and English for clarity.

Scots:

Some hae meat and canna eat, And some wad eat that want it, But we hae meat and we can eat, Sae let the Lord be thankit.

English:

Some have food and cannot eat, And some would eat that lack it, But we have food and we can eat, So let God be thanked.

Pictish Cross Slab

Drinks

- **Bouvrage.** A natural raspberry drink made in Alloa, Scotland with the aim of making available the taste of fresh raspberries all year round. The juice of one pound of Scottish Raspberries is put into every 750 ml bottle. It's slightly sparkling, not too sweet, and non-alcoholic.

- **Cider.** This is my drink of choice in any pub, as I prefer the sweet stuff. Cider in America, traditionally, is a thicker, cloudy version of apple juice, and non-alcoholic. In the UK and Ireland, cider is light, carbonated, and alcoholic. It ranges from dry to sweet, and available in just about any pub I've ever been to. It is just beginning to gain some traction in the US, I see it in some grocery stores and on some restaurants' menus.

- **Bovril.** This is sort of like a fortified, spiced broth, which can be served as a drink, as well as being added like concentrated stock to flavor soups and stews. It's also spread directly onto bread, like Marmite and Vegemite.

- **Irn Bru.** An almost neon orange carbonated soft drink. It leaves a warm tingling on the tongue like strong ginger ale. I must say that Irn Bru is an acquired taste. The first taste I loved, not so much after that. It tastes (to me) as if someone made a soda out of orange Bubblicious gum. It is, supposedly, named after the drink that iron workers would have after their shift, Iron Brew became Irn Bru. It is also one of the few sodas that outsell Coca-Cola in its area.

- **Whisky.** Ah, what can I saw about whisky that isn't covered ad nauseum in many, many other books? Other than to say that whiskey (with an 'e') is Irish, while whisky (without the 'e') is Scottish. See more information below, at "The Whisky Trail."

- **Heather Ale.** This drink dates to the 17th century, *leann fraoich*. As distillation became more widely spread, nearly anything aromatic was sampled in the process, including wild heather.

- **Drambuie.** The word Drambuie is an old Scots Gaelic phrase, dram buidheach, meaning "the drink that satisfies." While the exact origin of this beverage isn't clear, one thing is that the MacKinnon clan has had one hand or another in the making since around the 18th century, after the Battle of Colloden. The first commercial sales of the drink came in 1910 in Edinburgh. By 1916, it was the first liqueur to be allowed in the cellars of the House of Lords, and shortly thereafter enjoyed worldwide distribution.

The Whisky Trail

While I shan't get into the debate as to whether Scotch Whisky or Irish Whiskey is better (as I prefer cider), there is plenty to see if you are a fan of the golden nectar.

Many of Scotland's distilleries were established on Speyside, among the northern foothills of the Grampian Mountains. Eight of these distilleries, Benromach, Cardhu, Dallas Dhu Historic Distillery, Glenfiddich, Glen Grant, The Glenlivet, Glen Moray, Strathisla, and Speyside Cooperage, and one cooperage (barrel makers) have come together under the banner of "The Malt Whisky Trail." This offers visitors to the area the opportunity to experience first-hand the history and the process behind the production of one of the world's greatest drinks. All the distilleries listed are open to the public and there are details of each distillery.

If you are in another area of Scotland, never fear! There are plenty of distilleries around the country, including those on the Isles of Islay, Skye, Mull, and Orkney, as well as Edinburgh and many other spots. Whisky truly does give a sense of national pride and is part of the Scottish national identity.

Around the early 12th century, using practices from the ancient Greeks, Babylonians and medieval Arabs, wine was fermented by the Italians.

This became incredibly popular in the medieval monasteries and was used as the base for many medicines.

The art of this distillation process was spread to Ireland and Scotland (and many other places) by monks establishing new monasteries. The process moved to a secular setting by The Guild of Surgeon Barbers, medical practitioners of the time.

The first evidence of whisky production in Ireland was in 1405, at Clonmacnoise.

The death of a chieftain was blamed on "taking a surfeit of *aqua vitae*" at Christmas. Scotland joined the party by 1494, where an order of malt was sent "To Friar John Cor, by order of the king, to make *aqua vitae.*"

Uisce beatha (ish-ka bah) is the Gaelic word for Water of Life. It was anglicized to whiskey in countries with an E in their name (such as the United States or Ireland), and whisky to those without an E, such as Canada or Scotland.

Drying Peat

PLANS AND MECHANICS

When you plan a trip somewhere, there are all sorts of facets to your planning. Each facet requires your attention, and ignoring one could be potentially upsetting, inconvenient, or worse. This section should help with the practical aspects of planning and enjoying a trip to Scotland. Here are some of the things I shall cover:

How do I plan a trip to Scotland? When do I go?
How much will it cost? Where will I stay?
How will I get around? What shall I visit?
What if something goes wrong?

Many people dream about the magic of Scotland. However, many do not grab this dream, why not? "It's too expensive," you say. "I could never afford a trip to Europe."

Less expensive than a week at Disneyworld, I say. For six people on a three-week Scotland vacation in June (2008), including airfare, rental car, B&B accommodation, and trip insurance, we spent about $2,600 per person. Yes, that's it. Now, this doesn't include food, petrol (gasoline) or souvenirs, of course, but it did include a wonderful vacation to a *truly* magical place.

Keep in mind that prices change all the time, especially for airfare. Any information I publish on hard airfare numbers will be obsolete by the time you read it, but I can and will give examples below.

So, how do you get such a deal? Well, it takes patience, research, and the ability to make decisions when you need to. I will take you through, step-by-step, how to get the best deal for a Scottish vacation.

DECISIONS: Why, Who, What, Where, When, and How

Why?

You should start by thinking about WHY you want to go to Scotland. Do you want to touch the roots of your ancestors? Or experience an ancient culture? Have you always felt an unexplainable pull? Or do you just want to get away from the screaming kids, or make your co-workers jealous? There are many reasons WHY you may want to go to Scotland. No need to pick one. Pick several! Use these reasons to help plan your trip.

Who?

WHO's going? You? Your spouse? Your children or parents? Your best friend? A huge group of twenty friends? This decision makes a big difference in accommodation and transportation choices. I have learned, through trial and many errors, that certain people travel well together, and some don't.

For instance, I will no longer travel with a mixed group of friends, spouse, and/or family. I have determined, to keep my sanity, that I shall only travel with one type of companion at a time. Otherwise, I become a funnel through which all complaints about others are poured. Choose wisely to avoid problems.

What?

WHAT to do? Are you interested in touring the whisky distilleries? Ruined or restored castles and abbeys? Cities or charming villages? Your trip doesn't have to have a theme, of course, but it is more fun if you do, and helps you to plan when your mind is a blank. Perhaps you've seen a movie or read a book set in Edinburgh, and want to visit the area? Or you dance and want to learn the Highland Fling, or you play an instrument and want to learn how to play the bagpipes? There is so much to see and do in Scotland that your imagination can take flight.

Where?

WHERE to go, of course, depends on WHAT you are doing. It also ties into WHEN you want to go. It probably needs to be considered as a package deal, so to speak.

WHERE includes the character of place: Towns and villages, or bustling city? Mountains or patchwork hills? Coastline or lochside? Each city has its own character, and a variety of places to stay, from historic B&Bs to luxury hotels. Scottish cities are compact so choose an accommodation with parking, as you won't need the car, as most things are within walking distance. Villages used as a base of exploration can be wonderful, and you get more chances to meet the locals.

Urban, suburban, or rural, you will be spoiled for choice! More details on this decision are explored under "WHY?" below.

The Minch

When?

WHEN is an important consideration. While the weather is, on average, nicer in the summer, and the days are longer, the trip will also be more expensive and more crowded. Alternatively, while the winter is cheaper and you have things more to yourself the weather is harsher, most traditional tourist attractions will be closed or some natural sites inaccessible in poor weather, and the days will be much shorter (an average of seven hours of daylight in fair weather). It is up to you to determine your comfort zone.

The peak season for Scottish travel is June, July, and August. The shoulder seasons of March, April, and May, and September, October, and November may offer the best of both worlds, and is my preferred time for traveling. Except for right around Christmas and Easter, the winter months, December through February, offer the best deals, but also the highest possibility of weather difficulties and limited open attractions.

How?

HOW are you going to get there, and HOW will you get around once you are there? Usually, the easiest answer to the former question is via airplane. Airfare will be a good chunk of your travel budget, but with some research and patience, you can find a decent fare.

Keep in mind that some websites quote the base fare with taxes, and then have additional fees, so make sure you are comparing apples to apples when doing your research. While there are now regulations set to have the total fare (including taxes) displayed, that won't include baggage fees and other optional add-ons.

There are several sites I search for comparable flights, such as the airlines themselves, but also Kayak and Googleflights. The cost is usually higher from smaller airports, and from those farther away, such as California, as compared to east coast departures. And check the most direct flights to save on travel time and fewer connections. Example: California to London Heathrow to Edinburgh, total flight time around fifteen hours. Return the same route and you can clear Customs at Heathrow.

The latter question, of how to travel once you are on the ground, has more options. While my favorite, by far, is to rent my own car and wander around the moors and hills on my own, this is not the only option. You can travel to some of the main destinations by train or even by ferry or go via tour bus (either an all-inclusive tour or shorter day trips). You can also hike or cycle. You can even combine methods of travel, example: Drive to Oban and get the ferry to the Isles of Iona and Mull.

Since COVID-19, costs of many things have gone up, so everything is still in flux. Rental cars have skyrocketed due to companies selling off excess inventory during the pandemic. I recommend researching early, reserving early, and keep checking to ensure you have a good deal.

Renting A Car

The first thing to remember is that all rentals have compulsory insurances included in the rental rate. These minimum insurances include

CDW (Collision Damage Waiver), VTP (Vehicle Theft Protection), LLI (Limited Liability Insurance), and location surcharges, as well as the cost of the rental itself and VAT (Value Added Tax).

Understand what each of these insurances pay and consider optional insurances on collection, which include PLI (Personal Liability Insurance), SCDW (Super CDW), TPI (Third Party Insurance), and T&WC (Tyre/Tire and Windscreen/Windshield Coverage).

CDW covers damage to the vehicle. Period. If you're in an accident, this compulsory insurance repairs or replaces the vehicle (most CDW coverage only pays up to 80-90% of damages and the renter covers the balance).

SCDW is the same as CDW but covers that percentage which is left over from traditional CDW coverage. This covers 100% of the vehicle.

If you're in an accident and there are injuries, LLI will pay medical costs for those injured if you hit another vehicle. It will not pay for those injured in your vehicle. PLI covers injured passengers in your vehicle.

CDW/SCDW and LLI/PLI are often covered as part of your travel insurance package. If they are, you do not have to buy them again as part of the vehicle rental contract. Be sure to bring a copy of your travel insurance with you for proof upon vehicle collection.

T&WC is not compulsory insurance but one you should consider adding on. As part of the standard rental contract, if you puncture a tire or a stone cracks the windscreen, you are responsible for repair, which can be as much as £100 for a tire and £500 for the windscreen. Adding T&WC onto your contract will pay these damages so you don't have to.

Read the fine print when getting rental quotes online. Some companies do include more than the basic insurances in their quote.

Most credit cards issued in the US will cover travel insurance on vehicles rented in Scotland. However, many of them have a value cap of $50,000 for the rented vehicle (this largely applies to luxury models). Depending on the size of car you rent and the exchange rate that day, it may be that the car you rent is over that cap, and thus the credit card will not cover it. Also, cars might be more expensive there than the same car would be here. Be prepared!

If you do not have travel insurance coverage on your credit card, you might be able to buy it as part of your travel insurance. Check out *Insure My Trip* online to see your options.

Iona

Also, if you get coverage from someone other than the rental company, be aware they may put either a hold on your credit card for several thousand pounds, or charge a deposit to the card, which is refunded when you return the car in good order. While this sounds like the same thing, it is not, as many credit cards charge a 2-3% foreign transaction fee for any transaction. This would be charged twice for a deposit and a subsequent refund, so you would be out this fee twice. Do some research ahead of time to see if this is the policy of the rental agency, their rules can change at any time.

RESEARCH:

Find out everything about everything, then throw half of it away.

The internet is many things. Addicting, yes; maddening, yes. But it is also incredibly helpful when doing research, especially about places far from your home. Airfare, accommodation, car rental, and destinations like cities, beautiful beaches (yes, they exist in Scotland), and gloomy castles are all listed somewhere, you just need to find them. The best order of research I've found is as follows:

- Make up a crazy wish list, anything you (and your traveling companions) have any interest in seeing.
- Decide which items are your "must-sees," those places you have your heart set on.
- Plot out these "must-sees" on a map of Scotland.
- See if you can construct a basic progressive itinerary from those spots, incorporating the non-"must-sees" when you can, trying not to double back on yourself.
- See if you can find airfare in and out of places logical for the itinerary.
- Research accommodation along the way.
- Research ground transportation.

The airfares available may define your itinerary somewhat, and the itinerary will help define other items. Just try staying flexible.

Itinerary

There is a wealth of information online about places to see: castles and manor houses, museums and historical monuments, special interest workshops, battle sites, and many other places of interest. Most cities and towns, even villages, have their own website with tourist information. In addition, many travel agent websites have great information for the intrepid traveler. Even more, there are websites dedicated to those interested in travel, with wonderful forums for those odd questions. Some of my favorites are listed in the Maps and Resources section at the back of this book.

Once you have done exhaustive research of the places you want to see, throw half of it out. Yes, that's right, you will likely end up with a list of seventeen things to see in each location, but you will only have time for a third of them, so pick your favorites. I usually list about twice as many as I can possibly see and bold the ones I REALLY want to see. That way, if, for some reason, I have extra time (say, one of my must-sees was closed, or didn't take as long as I had thought it would), I can see some of my second-string choices.

Also, do yourself a favor by leaving room in your itinerary for free time, wandering around and getting lost, people-watching at a café, or just having a pint with the locals. These are usually the most memorable parts of your trip, so leave time for them.

You don't want to end up with an itinerary where you are rushing through things so fast you don't see them. I call this the Plaid Blur Tour. While some people prefer a fast-paced vacation, it does sometimes pay off to stop and enjoy what you are seeing, rather than just marking off things you've seen on a checklist, like the Griswolds in *European Vacation*. Edinburgh Castle? Check! Loch Ness? Check!

If you've got the places listed you want to see, look for a pattern. Are they all close to a central location? If so, pick places where you can stay multiple nights and use them as bases of exploration around those regions.

Or can they be strung together in a circle over a larger region? If so, spend a couple nights in each place, moving around that circular route.

Be visual, pay attention to road maps, plan wisely, and try to avoid crisscrossing or backtracking. Check driving times between places with Via Michelin or Google Maps. Then add about 25% to those driving times, as mapping programs don't consider Scottish roads. They twist and turn, which can keep speeds down lower than the actual posted speed limit. There are hills and valleys, sheep and cattle, tractors, and tour buses, and even road works. You don't want to spend all your time driving, trust me. It gets very tiring, especially as you will likely be driving a manual transmission, which are the majority rental cars available (automatics are available at a higher cost).

I try keeping my driving time to around three hours at the most and break it up with stops at attractions along the way.

I find the most reliable way to figure a distance and time is to multiply the miles by 35mph to get an average travel time. Example: If I need to travel fifty miles to my next accommodation, at the average speed limit of 35 mph, the drive alone will take approximately an hour-and-a-half. Add onto this time, the time it takes to get to attractions, then add some additional time for stopping for lunch, photo opportunities, and exploring the side streets and quaint shops. What does that sign say? Let's see where it goes!

If you enlist in a travel agent to help you design an itinerary, be sure to ask about the agent's personal experience in Scotland. It's quite common for agents to sell custom itineraries but never having visited Scotland themselves and thus do not have any real experience. Be sure to work with a professional who specializes in Scottish travel and has hands-on experience and knowledge as a local would.

Edinburgh

Airfare

This is usually the biggest chunk of your travel budget. There is a definite season to vacations in Scotland, summer. While many people do go on the "peak" months of June, July and August, there is indeed a reason why summer is the best. The days are longer to see sights, warmer weather, less rain and wind, and everything is open. This also means the airfare is the most expensive, as well as hotels. Smaller accommodation, like B&Bs and guesthouses, have much the same rates year-round.

The shoulder months of March, April, and May, and September, October, and November are becoming more popular, as the weather is still usually decent, and the days aren't incredibly short yet. However, this also means the airfares are creeping up as these become more popular times to travel. Please note some places won't be open in the shoulder and off seasons, many B&Bs, some restaurants, and most attractions may close after October and remain closed until mid-March. If you are in doubt, check the attraction's website first to see if your "must-see" sights are open before making definitive plans. Most sites list daily opening hours and when they close for the season.

When I've decided on what I want to see and where I want to stay, I look for the most convenient airport(s), then I start researching my flights. I go to dozens of websites, sometimes daily, to watch fares before buying. When I've visited Scotland, I found good fares on a one-day fare sale through United Airlines, which I only knew about due to a Fare Alert email I had signed up for. The fare was gone in an hour, but I'd pounced on it and got it. Do your research. There are deals out there.

Also consider flying into one city and out of another. This is great for Scotland, as you can fly into Edinburgh, explore up the east coast, and fly out of Glasgow at the end of your trip. This is called an open-jaw ticket, and usually doesn't cost much more, if any, than a normal round-trip ticket. Keep in mind, though, that Glasgow and Edinburgh are only one hour's drive from each other, so it may not be a huge savings in time. There are shuttles available to take you from one airport to the other for a reasonable price. We used one on our trip, landing in Glasgow, and then taking a bus which transported all six of us to our front door in the Edinburgh flat we had rented (about an hour- and-a-half drive). Total cost, about £100.

There are others, of course, but these are the ones I've used most often. Also don't forget to check the airline websites; if you find a great fare on Expedia for Delta, Delta might have it cheaper on their own site, and it is usually better to deal directly rather than through a middleman. Some airlines, like Southwest (which isn't international, but could get you to a hub like New York cheaper) may not be listed on price consolidation sites like Travelocity, Kayak, or Expedia. Check those sites separately.

I sign up for airfare alerts when I'm researching fares, so I get quick notification of sales. Airfarewatchdog can keep track of a particular fare, as the site follows fare's rise and fall. You can set up email alerts for when the price rises or drops a particular amount or to a particular level. Some of the consolidation websites do this as well.

When you buy your tickets, check out the cancelation policies. Usually, the cheaper the flight, the less flexible the changes allowed. Make sure you are going before you purchase non-refundable, no-change tickets.

If you have any reason why you might not be able to make the flight, either pay extra for flexible tickets, or get travel insurance that covers flight cancelation. Some fares cover delays or cancelations due to medical reasons, for instance. Keep in mind they usually mean YOUR medical reason, not a child or a parent for whom you need to stay to take care of. Airlines are very strict about cancelations so be sure to read the fine print before buying your tickets.

Dunvegan Castle

Accommodation

Bed & Breakfasts and Guesthouses

Once you have your airfare and itinerary, you know which nights you need accommodation and in which locations.

Scotland is wonderfully full of adorable bed & breakfasts; I highly recommend this accommodation choice. The B&Bs in the US tend to be more upscale and expensive than those in the Scotland, so don't go by their example. Most B&Bs I've ever been in have been comfortable, clean, cozy, and a delight to stay. B&Bs around the countryside run around £40 per person sharing per night (pppn or pps) and include the traditional full Scottish breakfast. You will pay higher for city guesthouses. Where B&Bs are generally family homes, larger guesthouses are purpose-built B&Bs with higher occupation numbers, perhaps more amenities, and a more extensive breakfast menu, and will have a slightly higher cost.

If you are staying in the city, and have more than just a couple people, it may be more economical to rent a flat (an apartment). We had six in Edinburgh and rented a lovely two-story flat just a block off the Royal Mile. It had a total of four bedrooms, had the original wood floors from the 15th century, vaulted ceilings, and a lovely wooden four poster bed! The dining room was a bit claustrophobic, for all it looked like a medieval dining hall, and the clothes washer and dryer were compact, but it was a great place to get our bearings, and a short walk to the medieval heart of the city.

Hotels

Hotels usually charge by room rather than per person but are based on two people sharing. Many usually do not include breakfast in the deal, referred to on booking as "room only." Hotels are usually more cookie-cutter and sterile. A Hilton is the same in San Francisco as it is in New York, London, and Japan, and they lack the authenticity of a family-run B&B. In my opinion, hotels are a place to stay based on convenience rather than a place to enjoy. However, there are some small family-run hotels in rural areas which may offer you the privacy you want while also adding something interesting to your overall visit to Scotland.

Many old country houses have been converted to guesthouses and small hotels, which would add interest to your stay in the region, especially if the accommodation has any historic ties to local history.

You can also find castle hotels around the country, such as Culcreuch Castle in Stirlingshire, or Dalhousie Castle near Edinburgh. Prices in these types of accommodation are generally more expensive but would certainly add something special to your trip, especially if you're traveling to Scotland for a special event, like an anniversary or honeymoon.

Hostels and Other Specialist Accommodation

Hostels (both regular hostels and youth hostels), camping, caravanning (RV), canal boats, colleges offering dormitory rooms for the summer, are other options for creative accommodation. There is no end of unusual places to stay. Some hostels in Scotland are part of old castles, such as Castle Rock Hostel. There are some churches and monasteries that are now B&Bs. Get creative!

Self-Catering

Self-catering houses are also an option, especially if you have a large group or prefer the privacy of a "home from home" type of accommodation. The biggest downfall is many require a seven-day minimum stay, usually from Saturday to Saturday. Some are willing to rent out for short breaks, so always check.

Once you have decided where you want to stay, make a reservation. Make sure to check the cancelation policies with all accommodation you book. Most B&Bs and guesthouses require at least 24-hour cancelation, and many hotels can be canceled the morning of arrival.

However, self-catering and specialty accommodation usually have a four-to-six-week cancelation period for a full refund. The time you cancel will dictate how much of your money you get back! Inside that four-to-six-week period means staged refunds, with service charges increasing the closer to your reservation date.

Email is usually the normal option for communication these days. I prefer this method as it leaves a "paper trail," and I make sure to bring a copy with me. Not everyone in Scotland is web-savvy, even if they have a website, so be patient. Some may require a phone call, most will require a credit card to secure bookings, even if it's not charged. This protects the establishment against "no-shows."

Don't forget the time difference. Scotland is ahead of Eastern Standard Time by five hours, and by eight hours from Pacific Standard Time. Noon in New York and 9am in San Francisco is 5pm in Scotland. If you're organizing your trip in the evening after work, remember the folks in Scotland could be asleep.

When booking your accommodation, not all places in Scotland are going to take credit cards. Those which do probably don't take American Express. None of them take Discover. Those which take credit cards will take Mastercard and Visa. Some are cash only, EVEN if they take a card number for the reservation. Be prepared to pay cash on departure.

If a host is going to take a deposit or take the full amount on booking, remember you will see a foreign transaction fee on your statement. Again, check the cancelation policy if you expect a refund on cancelation.

Scottish Traffic Jam

Ground Transportation

My recommendation for getting around Scotland is by renting a car. Exceptions would be if you are under or over the age limit for rentals, or maybe you have physical limitations, or if you are staying in a major city, like Edinburgh or Glasgow where you won't need a car because the city is compact enough to walk and parking is hard to find and expensive.

In the countryside, though, while it is possible to use buses and trains to get around, and certainly many people do, you won't find this an easy option, as it requires a lot of flexibility in your schedule. ScotRail travels between cities and major towns, but a vast part of the country has no rail travel at all. Getting to villages and remote attractions can be difficult to impossible and very time-consuming.

If you are in an organized bus tour, you are obliged to stick to that itinerary, so you can't make a detour on a whim to go find a hidden castle when you see a sign. You can't stay longer at one spot unless you want to get left behind. There is no flexibility with organized tours.

If you travel by public bus, you do have some flexibility in your itinerary, but you will be reliant on the bus schedule, which is often inconsistent for arrival and departure times.

Now, I know it is scary to think about driving on the "wrong" side of the road, but it's not really that difficult, especially if you're a good, conscientious driver by nature. It's not so bad as you think, and you will get used to it very quickly. The mind has an incredible ability to "mirror" and allow you to perform the same tasks, as if mirroring the motions to what you're used to.

It helps to have a designated navigator, as the signage in Scotland is a little different from what you may be used to. Signs tell you name of the next town, in English and in Scottish (Gaelic), as well as the route number and the distance in miles to other towns on that route. This means you should know the major towns on the way to where you are going, or even the ones just beyond your destination.

While national signs can be in both English and Gaelic, keep in mind that the more north you get into the Highlands, the signs might only be in Gaelic, so learn the local name of the places.

Most folks have map apps on their smartphones. If you don't, or if you don't have a data plan that you can use abroad, you a GPS can still be very helpful, and not only does it help you find places (IF you have a good address for the place, not always a given, especially in rural areas). It can definitely help you find your way BACK to your B&B if you deliberately get lost during the day, just for the fun of it. Most car rental companies offer them now, some of them even give them for free.

Big cities in Scotland don't require a car to get around. In fact, having a car is a liability in Edinburgh. It is difficult to get around with the heavy traffic, find parking is challenging unless you know where the few multi-story parking lots are, and it can be expensive both on the street and in the multi-story.

Edinburgh and Glasgow both have decent public transportation systems, and both cities are quite walkable. Smaller towns and villages, even those like Perth and Inverness, are very walkable as well, so parking for the afternoon and exploring the town on foot is usually the best option. For the bigger cities, if it's your final stop before returning home, turn in the car before getting to the city, or wait to rent it until you leave to begin your holiday.

Gasoline is called petrol in Scotland (gas is the natural stuff pumped into your home) and is very expensive. At the time of this publication, the cost is running around $8 USD per gallon. Yes, really! The good news is you can usually get around 45 mpg from economy size cars (larger cars get slightly lower miles per gallon).

Filling up a tank can still run you $100 or more, so budget accordingly. Remember the itinerary you made with estimated driving times? Use that mileage and double it. Yes, double it. You will be going to places, taking day trips, going out for dinner, stopping at brown sign sites, all sorts of side trips.

I've gotten decent deals from AutoEurope and from Enterprise Rental. I would advise against renting from a place you've never heard of. Cars can be very expensive, and it's difficult to fight a fraudulent damage claim from overseas. Having said that, there are several privately owned rental companies who have been in business as long as fifty years.

See more on the details and problems of renting a car above in the GROUND TRANSPORTATION section.

OTHER CONSIDERATIONS

Okay, you've done your research, gotten your airline tickets, made your reservations for accommodation, and your car rental. Ready to go? Not yet!

Travel Insurance

You break your leg the week before the trip. Ruined! All your money lost! Not so, Grasshopper, if you bought the proper travel insurance. Go to Insure My Trip and compare the benefits of different packages. Find out if your own health insurance will cover you on foreign soil (some credit cards also have built-in travel insurance).

Look for things like cancellation insurance in case of medical emergency, reimbursement for lost luggage, additions to the above-mentioned car insurance, etc. Compare the benefits between what you already pay for and what you need to travel and find a travel plan which fits right for your needs. For a small investment, you get a great deal of peace of mind.

Sound of Mull

Passports and Visas

All most people need to travel to Scotland is a valid passport from their country of origin. Also, be sure there are no impediments that would cause you to be refused entry, such as a felony record. This should be taken care of before you even buy your tickets. Normal processing times for a new passport is six weeks, but please give it plenty of leeway (especially if you've already bought non-refundable tickets). This can increase to about twelve weeks without notice. Don't procrastinate. My husband ended up getting his passport the morning we flew out, we were very nervous, to say the least.

US citizens don't need visas for visits of up to ninety days in Scotland, but if you are going somewhere else or staying longer, do read up on the requirements long before your flight, and make sure all paperwork is in order.

Starting in 2024, there is a new law called ETIAS (European Travel Information and Authorisation System), which requires visas from some previously exempt countries. This doesn't apply to Scotland, but if you are traveling to other countries as part of your trip, do some research to see if this affects you.

Money

Scotland uses the British Pound Sterling (£) for its currency. The exchange rate fluctuates every day, of course, but it tends to be somewhere between $1.20 and $1.40 per £1.

Cash

I recommend going to your bank and getting a couple hundred dollars' worth of sterling as travel money for the day you land. You can get more during your stay from the ATM, and/or use your credit card for purchases. You can also get some pre-trip sterling online through companies like AAA or Thomas Cooke or order it from your bank. Alternatively, larger airports have Bureau de Change desks where you can exchange your money for sterling. Keep in mind the exchange rate is higher in the airport for this convenience.

Travelers Checks

NEVER travel with large amounts of cash. Travelers' checks were an option for many years, but now, you'd be hard pressed to find anyplace that accept or exchange them. Just... don't.

ATMs in Scotland

Be sure your bank is part of the LINK system to access your account in Scotland. Also, you will not be given a choice between linked accounts. Your ATM card will only have access to your primary account from Scotland, which is often your checking account.

You may wish to save hassle while in Scotland by opening a dedicated travel account and getting a new ATM card for that account, and make sure all travel funds you wish to access are in that account.

Some smaller towns and villages won't have an ATM. You may have to travel to a larger town nearby to get cash. I've also noticed some ATMs (often the only one) are inside stores, so if the store is closed, so is access to cash. However, as more gas stations open which are parts of small convenience shops, small ATMs in the back of the shops are often installed. Plan accordingly if you're traveling in a remote area, banks might be closed after 4pm weekdays and all day on the weekends, and in the remotest areas, may only be open a few hours a day.

Calanais II

Credit Cards

Be sure to contact your bank prior to traveling to let them know to expect charges made in Scotland during your travel dates. This will, hopefully, save you the hassle of having your card put on hold, or worse, canceled, mid-trip and leaving you without your card. Some cards offer an online tool to enter travel dates.

Sometimes their fraud department will still put a hold on, but a phone call can often clear this up.

If you don't have a credit card, or your interest rate is too high, shop around for a card with a good rate. Many (Capital One is one of the few which don't) add on an extra 2% for any foreign transaction, in addition to the 1% Visa/MC charges.

You don't want to carry too much cash with you, but some B&Bs, while preferring cash even if they take credit cards, require reservations made guaranteeing the booking with a credit card to protect them against "no-shows."

Before you travel, you can also set up a prepaid debit card that is based on sterling and use it throughout the trip, including getting cash from the ATM. I've heard of some issues with American credit cards that use six-digit PINs in the UK which only uses four digits. Be sure your card uses a four-digit PIN and avoid those problems.

The UK (including Scotland) has a chip and pin format for all credit cards and laser/ATM cards. While the machine in most shops takes both chip and pin and swipe cards, shop staff may not have been trained how to use the swiper or how to manually enter the card number. You may need to ask for a manager to complete your charge.

Packing

Sure, you've packed dozens of times for vacations. What's the big deal? Well, the flight luggage restrictions for carry-on and checked luggage, for one. Airlines have lots of rules, so it behooves you to know them before you get to the airport.

Carry-ons: Most airlines have their carry-on rules on their websites. Some have weight as well as size restrictions. Airlines differ, but you may find your carry-on must fit under the seat in front of you, even if you intend on putting it in the overhead compartment, and it must not weigh more than around fifteen to twenty pounds.

Liquid restrictions also need to be obeyed. Check before you go. Right now, any carry-on liquids must be in containers no larger than 3oz

(100ml) and they must all fit comfortably in a quart-sized clear Ziploc bag. Liquids include gels and semi-solid things roll-on deodorant and toothpaste, so do be careful. When in doubt and you absolutely don't need it for your flight, check it in your luggage or leave it at home.

Jackets and medical equipment (like CPAP machines) are not counted toward your carry-on limits, though cameras and laptop computers are. I've taken heavy things from my carry-on and put them in my purse, which is rarely weighed. You can also stuff the pockets of the jacket. I packed some of my heavy electronic stuff, like chargers and batteries, into my CPAP machine case.

It's highly recommended you carry prescriptions with you rather than putting them in your checked luggage. In the event your luggage gets misdirected, you will still have your medication. Prescription medicines must be labeled in the traveler's name; be sure to get your doctor to write out a copy of your prescription and carry it with you. If you lose your medication, bring your prescription to a chemist to have refilled.

You may also find that if you're carrying baby food or formula that it may need to be tested at the gate. Where adult food is concerned, you will be asked at security to dispose of things like uneaten food, and open bottles and cans of water or colas. Visit the Transport Security Administration (TSA) website for lists of acceptable carry-ons and restrictions. This list will also help you to know what you can bring on board to entertain yourself or your kids, such as electronic games, music players, laptops, tablets, eReaders, etc.

The site will also provide you with information on things like knitting needles, crochet hooks, scissors, etc. Keep in mind that even if it's on the TSA acceptance list, it's purely up to the discretion of the officers at security. Don't bring your expensive needles and hooks in the event they're not allowed, and TSA requires you to throw them away.

Checked luggage: Some airlines charge hefty fees for overweight luggage and limit the number of pieces each person can check. While airline restrictions vary for long-haul flights into the UK, the maximum weight allowance is about fifty pounds, and some airlines can allow up to two fifty-pound suitcases per person.

Also, if you're in the habit of locking your suitcases, be sure to use TSA approved locks. If inspectors need to access your suitcases for any reason, they have a master key to open those locks, or they will cut off non-TSA locks to inspect. If there is an inspection, you'll know when you get home to unpack and find an inspection notice on top of your items. TSA approved locks are available in most travel sections in department stores and travel shops, as well as stores like Target, WalMart, etc.

Don't, don't, don't put valuables or medicines in your checked luggage! I cannot emphasize this enough, yet people do it every day. Cameras, laptops, anything fragile, anything essential, must go in your carry-on. They've even created a reality show based on people buying up abandoned and lost luggage, hoping for hidden treasure inside.

Tomb of the Eagles

Of course, this makes your carry-on heavy, so some decision-making is sometimes necessary, as you've seen above, there are strict weight limits for carry-ons. I usually put one day's worth of clean clothes in my carry-on, in case the checked luggage is delayed or lost. If you have something valuable, consider leaving it at home. Do you really need the diamond stud earrings on the trip, or will the cubic zirconia work? On my last trip, I did carry-on only for the sixteen-day trip.

Airlines have lost my luggage too many times in the past. On my trip to Scotland in 2008, my baggage was delayed for five days. Luckily,

I had a change of clothes and most of my required paperwork, so it was okay, even if annoying.

Bring a soft-sided carry-on or luggage, as it will likely expand with the things you buy on your trip. Some are expandable with zippered sides. Or just bring an extra duffel bag to check on the way back. It's much less annoying to wait five days for your dirty clothes to arrive home than it is for your clean clothes to arrive on vacation.

Jet Lag

The bane of travelers! Many people suffer from jet lag when they travel across time zones. If you are in the eastern US, you will be five hours ahead in Scotland. If you are from the western US, that increased to eight hours. While everyone's body reacts differently, here are some tips that I've followed or heard in the past that might help.

- **Hydrate.** Drink plenty of water during your flights. This helps keep your body functioning normally and reduces travel stress. Drinking alcohol can make the problem worse, so go easy on the cocktails, as they can dehydrate you.
- **Sleep.** If you can sleep on the overnight trip, do so. Even if it is only a couple of hours, this will help. I usually use earplugs and eyeshades to block noise and light. I try not to sleep very much the night before the flight, so I sleep better on the plane. Your mileage may vary!
- **Routine.** I tend to go to bed an hour earlier for each of the three days before my trip. For instance, if I normally go to bed at 10pm, I will go at 9pm three days before my flight, 8pm two days before, 7pm the night before, waking earlier each morning until the day of departure. That way, your body is a little more acclimatized to your new schedule, resulting in a smaller jolt once you arrive.
- **Activity.** When you do wake up, make sure to try to get some sunshine first thing! This wakes up your body and lets your circadian rhythm settle in. The day I arrive, I usually make sure to do things all day, and try to avoid napping (occasionally I give in, but make sure it's only an hour or two!). I don't plan anything heavy, like a two-hour drive or climbing a mountain. Light activity, some

sightseeing, walking around the town. Then I usually crash around 9pm, and sleep like the dead. The next morning, I'm bright-eyed and bushy-tailed, ready to tackle the world! Getting into your normal sleep pattern right away helps. Wake at your normal time and go to bed at your normal time. Even on arrival day.

- **Sugar levels**. Invariably, my husband has a sugar crash halfway through the second day of the trip. We keep regular mealtimes and top up with power bars to counter any problems. Your body goes through a lot of stress through travel, especially if you are older or have muscular/metabolic issues, such as diabetes or fibromyalgia. Plan accordingly and make sure you have supplies on hand to combat them.

Stenness Stones

READY TO GO? Don't forget the smile!

Don't forget to pack the most important thing for any trip, a great attitude. This small item can make the worst disaster into a hilarious story and get you through a difficult situation with authorities and can take the biggest lemon and make lemonade out of it. After all, how can it be terrible, you're in Scotland!

A trip to Scotland will be full of wonderful memories, historic experiences, and meeting wonderful folks. Whether you get addicted like I have or are happy with going once and treasuring the memory forever, you will have an exquisite time.

Scott Monument
Edinburgh

DISCOUNTS AND DEALS

Make no mistake, budgeting is difficult. When you are planning a trip anywhere, one of the first things you do is look at your budget for the trip. Sometimes this can be intimidating, and you are left trying to figure out how to get the most out of your limited funds and resources. This section is designed to help you find ways to stretch those resources and get the best vacation your money can buy.

Dunvegan Castle Garden

A lot of this will depend on when you go and how long you are going to stay. A week in January is going to be much less expensive than a week in August, especially if you are going to Edinburgh during the Military Tattoo and Festival month. Airfare will be higher during the peak season of June, July and August, a bit lower on the shoulder season (March, April, and May, and September, October, and November), and lowest during the winter months (except around Christmas which can be more expensive to travel than in August). While it doesn't vary as much (or as capriciously), higher end accommodations will also vary based on season. Some may even be closed during the winter months, so be warned and plan accordingly.

The most important aspect of finding the best deal is RESEARCH. You must spend some time searching for deals and know enough to realize it's a bargain before buying. This applies to airfare, car rental, accommodation, entrance fees, train tickets... whatever you are looking for. What is a good deal? Like anything, it depends on what you're willing to pay versus how much you really want it. But I can give you some guidelines via my past experiences.

Planning

One of the best things I would recommend is to visit the Undiscovered Scotland website. It has a fantastic interactive map that helps you to plan out your trip, with blurbs and pictures about all sorts of interesting spots. It shows you how close each is to the other and allows you to plan accordingly. This will cut down on the back-and-forth driving that you can easily fall victim to, saving on both time and petrol/gas expenses.

There are several discount cards that can help reduce the cost of entering many monuments and properties. Many museums are free, by the way. Take advantage of that! The Scottish Heritage Pass, Edinburgh Pass, Historic Scotland Pass, and National Heritage Membership all offer discounted entry into many of Scotland's historic attractions. Do some research. If you plan on visiting five or more of the sites they cover, it may be well worth the cost. Not all historic sites are covered, so do look them up.

I find a great way to get a good overview of the cities of Edinburgh and Glasgow, and to travel around the cities, is to get tickets for the hop-on/hop-off bus which winds through the streets, stopping at various attractions and offering commentary. A good way to find them is to look for the open-top buses. The closed ones are usually for local city travel, not tourists.

You do not need to pre-book these tours. Just show up at one of the stops, which are signposted around the city. Your ticket is good for twenty-four hours, so if you get on the bus at 1pm (the last tour out is a pick-up tour at 5pm), you can get back on the bus first thing in the morning for free and continue sightseeing until 1pm…though they may allow you the rest of the day if you get a nice driver.

I have enjoyed the hop-on/hop-off bus in many major cities, including London, Edinburgh, Dublin, New York City, Toronto, and Washington DC, and always find it to be entertaining and useful.

Also, I recommend the live commentary buses, as the canned ones tend to be less lively and lack humor. Each time I've gone, I manage to get a host who sings for us, not necessarily very well, but with great enthusiasm.

Isle of Lewis

Airfare

Usually, direct flights are less expensive, but that isn't always the case. Sometimes flying into or from a major hub, such as Newark or London, can help keep the costs down. Sometimes it's the only viable option. For instance, there are no direct flights from my closest airport to Scotland, I always need to fly to a larger airport that handles jets. The last trip, I had to fly from Jacksonville to Atlanta, to Manchester, to Glasgow. Check out the planning section for airfare for more information.

I use several tools for researching flights. Googleflights and Kayak are useful, though I usually purchase from the airlines themselves if I find a flight. I also sign up for email alerts from the airlines I might use, such as Delta or American. If you get notification of a great sale, and you know you are going, jump on it right away. That deal may be sold out in an hour!

I prefer to have control of my travel times, and most airlines require at least two hours layover on international flights for the connection. Anything less and your luggage may not arrive when you do. It is up to your personal level of comfort for chaos how you book your tickets.

If you are a student or a veteran, there are websites, such as Student Universe, STA Travel, or Veterans Advantage which can help you with better airfare.

Having enough frequent flyer miles with a particular airline (many credit cards allow you to accumulate these) can also either defray or replace the costs of a flight overseas. However, keep in mind many might have blackout periods, and sometimes seats are more difficult to get if you are using miles to obtain them. Some airlines allow you to apply your miles to a portion of the cost, reducing the total, no matter what the seat or flight.

Transportation
Renting a car is, by far, my highest recommended mode of transportation when traveling in Scotland. However simple this may

sound, it is fraught with peril and complexity, hidden charges and downright fraud. Please see my GROUND TRANSPORTATION advice in the previous section for lots of details on how to avoid, or at least minimize, them.

Another option is train travel. A Britrail pass may be helpful. However, the trains aren't quite as all-encompassing as traveling by car, and once you get to those hubs, you must find another way to travel around the enchanting countryside. Britrail travels between the cities and large towns but will not get you to the smaller destinations.

You could base yourself in one town or village and take daily private tours or a larger organize coach tour, or rent a horse-drawn caravan, cycle or hike, or just visit the town or village in a more relaxed local kind of way. It is all up to your style of travel, your budget, desires, and sometimes your physical limitations.

North Coast

Accommodation

While I'm in Scotland, I greatly prefer staying at Bed & Breakfasts as my accommodation choice. However, sometimes hotels are a better choice, such as the night before flying out of the airport, or in Edinburgh, where B&Bs aren't as available.

B&Bs can average £35-50 per person sharing per night (pppn) and include the famous traditional Full Scottish Breakfast. Specialty B&Bs

(historic houses, castle B&Bs, etc.) are usually a bit more expensive. I prefer B&Bs but occasionally splurge for a charming, historically significant place, or the odd thatched cottage.

Keep in mind this is pppn, and therefore, twice as much for two people in the one room. Single rooms are slightly higher, averaging £40-55 per night. Some B&Bs have family rooms at a discounted rate per person. Again, it depends on your personal level of comfort and sharing with your traveling companions. I have more information on accommodation in the previous section.

If you really want to splurge, you can always spend some time in a castle. Yes, you can find smaller castle accommodations than the five-star hotels. They are few but include some B&B accommodation and self-catering, and there's even a castle hostel.

What's the cheapest accommodation while traveling in Scotland? Camping out, of course! It's not my cup of tea, but plenty of people do it, especially if they have a bike or are hiking.

You can also try hostels for a great discounted stay. Youth hostels are no longer separate from other hostels, today's difference being average hostels and specialty hostels. In other words, age is no longer a defining factor to using a hostel. Typical hostels are purpose-built accommodation with shared dorms with shared bathrooms. Scottish Youth Hostels Association (SYHA) is a popular site for booking around the country.

Stromness

Another option, particularly for a large group, is a self-catering house. These are usually stand-alone houses or cottages, with a varying amount of space, for rent in usually week-long periods, most often from Saturday to Saturday. Sometimes, usually outside high season, you can get "short breaks" of two to three days instead.

Sometimes this is an option in the city, as well. We rented a two-story flat a block from the Royal Mile in Edinburgh, complete with brick arched ceilings, four-poster bed and the original 15th century hardwood floors. It had a vaulted ceiling in the dining room, 2 bedrooms downstairs, and a small one-bedroom flat above it (they could be rented out separately). The entrance was on Victoria Street at the base of the hill Edinburgh Castle sits atop. The upper flat had a door that led out to a terrace, with another stairway leading up to the Royal Mile. Very convenient!

There are several places to find self-catering lodges, but I recommend going through a well-known agent, such as Visit Scotland, Embrace Scotland, or Cottages & Castles UK.

Food

Food can be an expensive part of your trip, or a very cheap one, depending on your planning and habits. Staying at a B&B can be a big part of this, the enormous breakfast will keep you fueled into the afternoon or early evening, if you let it.

We often do this, and then grab a meal late in the day for about £10 per person. Then we may have a light supper at another pub or have takeaway. Sometimes, if we are out hiking or exploring, we just grab snack foods at the local grocery store to bring with us instead of stopping for lunch. Bread, cheese, and smoked salmon are delicious local options and are great in sandwiches made on the go.

Often, we have gotten hungry mid-afternoon, only to find that many full-service restaurants are closed at that time. They typically close after 2pm and don't reopen until 4 or 5pm for dinner, so plan accordingly. Some pubs will still serve food during that time and takeaways are often open as well.

Late night dining (after 8pm) has a similar problem, with the same solutions. I remember one night, having driven all day from near Inverness, we took the ferry across to the Orkney Islands, arriving around

8pm. We took a bit of time finding our B&B, and by the time we settled in, we were starved.

We asked the hostess if there were any food options, and she sent us to the one large town, Kirkwall, and recommended either the Chinese or Indian restaurant as the only ones open. We got there around 10pm, and it was delicious. The place seemed a bit like a ghost town, though, and it was even during a music festival.

If you are staying at a self-catering house, you will have a kitchen where you can prepare meals at home rather than paying for expensive meals at restaurants. Granted, you are then not offered your Full Scottish Breakfast from the B&B, but sometimes all you want is a bowl of cereal or some toast when you wake up. Some privately owned self-catering house owners will supply, at no extra cost, fresh eggs for your fridge (especially if they have their own chickens), or even the makings for a Full Scottish Breakfast for the length of your stay.

The Quiraing, Isle of Skye

Drink

Pints are larger in Scotland than in the US, so drink carefully. And a half-pint of beer or cider is about the same price as the same amount of soda, so enjoy your drink! Don't dare drink and drive, though. The penalties for such are high, and those roads are scary enough while you are sober. While you won't get points on your home driver's license, you may get arrested and the car impounded, which results in many costs.

If you don't wish to pay the pub price, you can always go to the off-license, purchase some pints, and take them to the B&B to enjoy. Of course, then you miss out on the pub culture!

Things To Do

In addition to the many places already discussed above, numerous galleries and museums in Scotland are free of charge, a great way to spend a day, especially if the weather isn't great. On finer days, many parks and gardens are free as well. You often can find local festivals and fairs to shop in, listen to music, sample food, and have a grand time with little to no cost. Of course, the landscapes are free to view, as are many historical landmarks!

Children

Sometimes it is very difficult to plan trips when you have children. Whether your kids are young children or rebellious teenagers, finding places which have enough to keep them interested and engaged can be quite a challenge. There is an excellent resource I discovered called Travel for Kids, which has sections for many places, including Scotland. There are lots of museums and exhibits that include interactive stuff for kids to enjoy, so keep an eye out for those. A day full of seeing ruined abbey after ruined castle after ruined abbey is enough to bore even many adults, much less children. And having cranky children does not help anyone enjoy their vacation.

Wi-Fi

Most hotels and many B&Bs have now started offering free Wi-Fi, though it is not always GOOD Wi-Fi, and some turn it off during the night hours. Many cafés have it, though, as will any McDonald's (not that I recommend going to McDonald's when in Scotland, despite it SOUNDING like a local place, when you have so many other great options). Libraries will also have access. Some entire cities now offer free Wi-Fi, so do some research ahead of time to plan.

Summary

Remember earlier when I said a trip to Scotland was less expensive than a trip to Disney? Our last trip to Scotland, which was twenty-three days in June, was about $4,000 for airfare, rental car, trip insurance, B&Bs, and food, per person. You can spend more than this on two weeks in New York City, or at Disney. And there are all sorts of ways you can trim your budget even more on your trip.

Clava Cairns

HIDDEN GEMS

I cannot list all the castles, abbeys, churches and other major attractions, there are many other places to find popular spots. What I've tried to do is find the unusual, unique, mystical, hidden places that are a little more off the beaten path. If I have included a major site, it is because there is a compelling reason that it is popular, such as a mythical connection.

I've not been to all these places myself, of course, but I have gotten lots of help from friends and other resources. A huge help was the website Undiscovered Scotland, which has interactive maps to help you find places. It's well worth some time if you're planning your own trip. Please enjoy!

Aberdeenshire

Aberdeenshire is chock full of castles, Pictish stones, and whisky distilleries. What more could you need! Aberdeen City itself is known as the Granite City, for all the granite buildings that sparkle in the sun after a good rain.

Aikey Brae Stone Circle

Though you must walk through a dense wood to reach it, this stone circle sits atop an open hill, and you might see some roe deer as you search for it. It is between the towns of Maud and Old Deer, on the summit of Parkhouse Hill. There is a bit of a climb, and parking is a bit tight, so be prepared. It is a complete circle of ten stones, with a larger recumbent (lying down) stone. This site dates back about four thousand years and was built by the local farming community that inhabited the hills. Do your best not to sing "Aikey-Brae-key heart" when visiting!

Bass of Inverurie

This small cemetery near Inverurie hosts a medieval motte and bailey dating from circa 1100 CE, which appears to be guarding the small cemetery. Robert the Bruce occupied this site up to 1308 when he defeated the Earl of Buchan at the Hill of Barra nearby, known as the Battle of Inverurie 1308. This is distinguished from the Battle of Inverurie 1745 which was part of a Jacobite uprising.

There is also a line of Pictish symbol stones, the ruined walls left over from a church, and a cairn marking the Jacobite Battle of Inverurie 1745. If you venture north of Inverurie, you can find another Pictish stone, called the Brandesbutt Stone, with detailed carvings and Ogham writing.

Braemar Castle

This restored keep is one of two very rare Scottish castles which are protected by star-shaped walls, the other is Corgarff Castle (see below), both of which happen to be in the Grampian Mountains, on opposite ranges.

Braemar Castle was built by John Erskine in 1628, 18th Earl of Mar, mainly as a hunting lodge, but also to counter the rising power of the Farquharson clan. The keep was sacked and burned by John Farquharson, known as the Black Colonel of Inverey, in 1689 during the first Jacobite uprising.

By 1716, the castle was forfeited to the Crown but eventually passed onto John Farquharson who purchased the site in 1748 who then leased it to the government as a garrison for Hanoverian troops. It served as a garrison until 1831 when the site was returned to the Farquharson clan. The property was fully restored by the 12th Laird of Invercauld who entertained Queen Victoria when she was visiting Braemar for a local event called The Gathering. Documents from 1800 also note the castle had a fully intact moat. And the walls are dated to the 18th century, a time when star-shaped fortresses were popular forms of defense across the British Isles.

The keep is reportedly inhabited by several ghosts, including a young woman who, believing herself abandoned by her newlywed husband, committed suicide. Other ghosts include a piper, and a young baby. The most infamous inhabitant is the Black Colonel of Inverey himself, John Farquharson, who has reportedly been seen in certain rooms, and his tobacco is often smelled in the rooms. The castle itself has a curtain wall, turrets, a round stair tower, and stone-vaulted rooms to explore. It includes a dungeon called The Laird's Pit.

Brandesbutt Stone

This is an unusual example of Pictish stone art in that it contains Ogham writing, which is usually found in Ireland. The Ogham spells out IRATADDOARENS, perhaps referencing Eddarrnon, an original spelling of the name of a local saint, St Ethernanus. This is a large stone that was once broken and used as a field boundary, but the pieces were found and reassembled. Nearby are the scant remains of a stone circle, the stones of which also turned up as part of the old boundary.

Cairn o' Mount

Legend has it that in the 11th century, Mac Bethad, commonly called Macbeth, survived the original English invasion but was wounded as he retreated with his men over the Cairnamounth Pass to take his last stand at the battle at Lumphanan in 1057 by Màel Coluim mac Donnchada. He eventually died from those wounds at nearby Scone, when his stepson, Lulach mac Gille Coemgàin, became king. This route over this pass was used many times through history as a passage back to England. This cairn dates from circa 2000 BCE.

Corgarff Castle

Nestled in the Grampian Mountains, this 16th century fortress is set inside a very rare 18th century star-shaped wall, the second of only two in Scotland (see Braemar above). In 1571, the place was burned which resulted in the deaths of Lady Forbes and her children, and many others in the keep. This incident resulted in the ballad, Edom O'Gordon. It's no doubt the castle must be haunted by all those ghosts. It was then used as a farmhouse from 1802 to 1827 as barracks from the time of the Jacobite uprising to 1831.

The most famous and last residents of Corgarff were the Ross sisters, known as the Castle Ladies. They occupied the keep until the First World War. After that time, the property went into the hands of Sir Edmund and Lady Stockdale who used the height of the walls as a shooting perch when out hunting. The Stockdale family eventually gave the castle to the Lonach Highland Friendly Society in 1979, and they fully restored it. Today, this castle has been restored and painted in traditional *harl* plaster, a type of lime rendering which has colored stones added which removes the need to paint, to give the appearance from afar of a rather squat, square castle that looked like one white box set on a larger white box. It looks very lonely and rather sinister in its isolation.

Craigievar Castle

A few miles south of Alford, this castle was built in the 1580s in an L-plan and has a traditional harled surface that looks like pink-colored plaster. This keep was the seat of Clan Sempill and the Forbes family for three hundred and fifty years until it was given to the National Trust of Scotland in 1963, when restoration began. Today, the site is open to the public and especially noted for its plasterwork ceilings, including recreated images of the Nine Worthies* and of Forbes family members. It has many turrets, gargoyles, and corbels to create a classic fairytale castle look, and is now open to the public. There is a massive iron portcullis, hearkening back to a more defensive age. There is a secret staircase, and the interior has been restored with furnishings dating to the 17th and 18th centuries.

*A note about Worthies: These figures are most often seen in churches and cathedrals and hold a sacred spot in the main nave. The Worthies are nine historical, scriptural, and legendary people who personified the ideals of chivalry as established in the Middle Ages, three Christians: Charlemagne, King Arthur, and Godfrey of Bouillon; followed by three pagans: Julius Caesar, Hector, and Alexander the Great; and lastly the three Jews: David, Joshua, and Judas Maccabeus.

By the late 14th century, Lady Worthies began appearing to accompany the Nine Worthies, though were not standardized, and varied by region.

Crathes Castle

If you have many castles in your plans, and fear burning out, this may be one you still want to see. Built first as a timber structure by the Burnetts of Ley on lands given to them by Robert the Bruce in 1323, this keep stayed in the same family for nearly four hundred years. The stone keep began construction in 1553 but was delayed several times due to issues with Mary, Queen of the Scots, though finally completed in 1596. A manor house extension to the keep was added in the 18th century.

Crathes is very well-preserved, especially the interior, which boasts original Scottish renaissance painted ceilings which survive in several Jacobean rooms, to include: the Chamber of the Muses, the Chamber of Nine Worthies, and the Green Lady's Room. It's the latter room where a green mist has been seen, which gives rise to the legend of the Green Lady.

Crathes is the only castle run by the National Trust to remain open all year. The estate has six hundred acres along the River Dee, including woodland and ponds, and some adventure sports such as a climbing wall. The walled gardens are especially lovely, covering nearly four acres. In 2004, excavations revealed a series of pits which were later analyzed to date back to 4000 to 8000 BCE, and possibly the oldest-known lunar calendar.

Cullerlie Stone Circle

Most stone circles are similar; Cullerlie is not. Most circles were built about four thousand years ago, and were believed to be astronomical in nature, and only much later cairns for the dead. Cullerlie, however, was built over thirty-five hundred years ago, and it has eight burial cairns inside the circle of eight standing stones, built concurrently. Seven of the eight cairns are surrounded by kerb stones. The avenue leading to the circle is lined by trees in a dramatic approach, despite the power pylon right next to the circle.

Dyce Symbol Stones

Located in the ruined kirk of St. Fergus, these two Pictish stones are carved with different symbols. The older of the two, carved in pink-red granite, has a swimming beast, a double disc, and a Z-rod. The later stone is a relief sculpture, entirely filled with interlacing carvings. There are four symbols around the cross, and some rare untranslated Ogham writing, the inscription on one stone reads:

EOTTASSARRHETODDEDDOTSMAQQROGODDADD

There has been no translation available but, typical of Ogham writing used mainly for memorials, it's thought this stone may have a personal name inscribed on it, MAQQ possibly meaning mac or son of, and ROGODDADD as the person's name. Perhaps: EOTTASSARR HETODDEDDOTS MAQQ ROGODDADD, or EOTTASSARR HETODDEDDOTS SON OF ROGODDADD. We may never know.

Easter Aquhorthies Circle

This recumbent stone circle is one of the best in existence. There are eleven upright stones with a low bank, to form a circle twenty-one yards in diameter. The stones may have been purposely chosen for their colors. The stones within the circle are pinkish in color, except the one next to the east flanker of red jasper. Both flankers are gray, while the recumbent is red granite.

Fyvie Castle

Some castles are impressive because of where they are built, like the cliffy heights at Stirling or Edinburgh. Others are impressive because of how they are built. Fyvie is one of the latter. Fyvie Castle dates from the

13th century, some sources claim William the Lion, aka William I, built it in 1211. Robert the Bruce held Fyvie as an open-air court, and Charles I lived there as a child. In 1390, following the Battle of Otterburn, the castle ceased being a royal stronghold and subsequently saw the possession of five successive families, each of whom added a new tower to the castle, Preston: the oldest tower, circa 1390-1433; Meldrum and Seton: twin tower entrance, circa 1599, and also years later, the great processional staircase commissioned by Seton; Gordon: circa 1178; and Leith: circa 1890.

Every castle seems to have a ghost legend, and Fyvie is no different. One story tells that during renovation work in 1920, the skeletal remains of a woman were discovered within a bedroom wall. The remains were laid to rest in Fyvie cemetery that day, but almost immediately, castle residents started complaining about strange noises and unexplained happenings. Fearing they had offended the dead woman, the remains were exhumed and replaced behind the bedroom wall. The hauntings ceased as quickly as they had begun. Another Fyvie mystery lies within a secret room in the south-west corner of the castle. Legend says it must remain sealed, lest anyone befell some disaster. There is also an indelible blood stain on a wall, and two ghosts and two curses are associated with Fyvie.

One of the curses has been attributed to 13th century nobleman, Thomas Learmonth, aka Learmount, Learmont, or Learmounth. He was not normally known by his birth name, however, but often called True Thomas, so named because he could not tell a lie. He was also known as Thomas the Rhymer, possibly for his gift of rhyming poetry.

Thomas was also a famous prophet who predicted the death of Alexander III in 1286, and predicted that a Scot would rule all of Britain, James I. Upon visiting Fyvie, a freak gust of wind is said to have shut the gates in his face, and he put the "curse of the weeping stones" on the place. Until three original boundary stones are removed from the area, there will always be succession problems. The first two were found, but the third is lost in the river Ythan.

Grampian Mountains

This isn't precisely a hidden spot, as it takes up a great swath of the countryside, but often people miss this stunning area, as they concentrate on Edinburgh and the Isle of Skye. The last time we traveled through, the browns, golds, purples, and grays jumped out at every sunspot, and whispered back into the earth when the clouds came. It was like the subconscious mind of an oil painter covering the landscape. Sheep jumped over streams and black lambs cavorted around (yes, really, cavorting!). Shaggy Highland Cows looked at us as we drove by. We stopped a couple times and just stood, stunned, looking at the landscape that surrounded us. Of course, we didn't stand long. The wind threatened to blow us away, in our hastily donned shawls and sweaters.

Loanhead of Daviot Stone Circle

While a belt of trees shelters most of the wind, nevertheless this circle, on the top of a hill, offers lovely views to the north and east. There are ten stones as well as a recumbent stone and flankers. As with most of these circles, the original purpose seemed to be astronomical, with a later purpose of a cremation cemetery, circa 1,500 BCE. The recumbent stone is two stones divided by a vertical cleft running their full length, which could have been some sort of fertility symbol, but was more likely to be the result of frost.

Maiden Stone

A Pictish stone with a distinctive notch near the top, the legend of this stone says that the daughter of the Laird of Balquhain made a bet with a stranger that she could make a good supply of bannock bread faster than he could build a road to the top of Bennachie. Her hand in marriage would be the prize, but the stranger was the Devil, and he won. She ran and prayed, so God turned her to stone. The notch is where the Devil grabbed her shoulder. The stone dates from circa 700 CE and is carved from a single slab of red granite which stands about three feet high that includes carvings of Celtic knotwork, motifs, and figures of people and animals.

Midmar Kirk Stone Circle

Unusual in its proximity to the church, this seventeen-meter stone circle has a recumbent stone with two flankers, which are eight feet long and sharp, looking a bit like demonic fangs. While some of the stones may have been moved when the church was built in 1787, and it's very likely a cairn was removed and destroyed in the process, the original stones appear to have been re-placed in other areas of the churchyard.

Museum of Scottish Lighthouses

Many people love and revere lighthouses, and this museum is a must-see for anyone with a tender heart for them. There are a huge number of lighthouses in Scotland, as the coast is treacherous and rocky. The museum itself showcases the variety of lighthouses, including models of all sorts, the collection of real lenses and lights, keys, semaphore flags, and keepers' uniforms. Scotland's first "official" lighthouse was built in 1787 here at Kinnaird Head, Fraserburgh.

Picardy Stone

One of the oldest and simplest of the Pictish carved stones, Picardy Stone dates to around the 6th or 7th century. It has three common Pictish symbols carved into the south face: a double disc and Z-rod, a serpent and Z-rod, and what looks like a polished bronze hand mirror which were common at the time. Nearby, at Dunnideer, there is a nearby that may have been linked to Picardy.

Rhynie Symbol Stones

Of the eight Pictish Symbol Stones found at Rhynie, the three most impressive are on display under a shelter near the parking lot at the Old Kirkyard. The largest depicts the head of an animal, possibly an otter or or seal, as well as traditional Pictish symbols of discs and Z-rods, which also adorn the other smaller stones. Some items found at the site also include Roman amphora from the 5th or 6th century, a Roman style jar with two handles and a narrow neck. Another can be found in a nearby field, uphill from the kirkyard. This may have been a settlement site for Pictish kings and can be visited by accessing a narrow single track into the valley of the Water of the Bogie, just outside Rynie village.

Rynie Man is a carving of a bearded man carrying an axe, on a six-foot-tall gabbro slab (a dark, coarse-grained plutonic rock of crystalline texture, consisting mainly of pyroxene, plagioclase feldspar, and often olivine). This stone was removed from its original location in Rynie and is now housed in Woodhill House, the headquarters of the Aberdeenshire Council.

Sunhoney Stone Circle

About a mile west of Echt is this recumbent stone circle. It is about twenty-seven yards in diameter, has nine stones plus a recumbent stone, with two flankers. This circle is aligned to the moon rise on the distant hillside. While it appears the original use of the stone circle stopped being used around 2000 BCE, excavations in 1865 suggest that the circle was repurposed to include cremation burials, and some small cairns were built inside the circle. Access is through a fenced field path and gate, and surrounded by a copse of trees, and is not signposted from the main road, making it a bit difficult to find. And it suggests the site has not been disturbed by agriculture or construction.

Angus

Aberlemno Stones

This is a series of five spectacularly carved standing stones in the village of Aberlemno. Three are on the side of the road in town, one in the kirkyard, and one thirty yards from the church. These stones have detailed carvings of Pictish origin, showing battles, beasts, serpents, disks, mirrors, and other symbols. Most of these symbols are of unknown meaning, though there are countless theories. One cross slab shows a battle won by the Picts, with the defeated Anglian army running away in defeat. This may represent the Battle of Nechtansmere from 685 CE. One is a Celtic cross-slab with both Pictish and Christian carvings on it. Before Celtic crosses were carved out (with holes between the arms and circle), they were carved on slabs like this.

Angus Folk Museum

This is a center for rural life and history near the village of Glamis. It was begun in the 1950s, and shows several terraced cottages, portraying life over the last two hundred years, as well as a Victorian schoolroom and authentic farm. You can experience life in an 19th century farm, witness the spinning and weaving, the agricultural wonders of a bygone age. All sorts of implements, furniture, and artifacts are contained in the homes. There is a bothy (small village) for the farm laborers, horses in the stables, and a working black smithy. There are various events held during the year, as well as a gift shop.

Arbroath Abbey

Founded in the 12th century for Tironensian monks, this abbey features distinctive red sandstone construction, making it glow in the afternoon sun. It was founded by King William I, as a memorial to the Archbishop of Canterbury Thomas Becket, his childhood friend. It has a unique triforium (open arcade) above the door. The abbey is famous mostly due to its association with the 1320 Declaration of Arbroath, wherein Scotsmen declared that they will always fight for freedom, even if only one hundred of them still live. Sir Walter Scott used the abbey as a basis for his description of the ruined monastery of St. Ruth in The Antiquary. The abbot's house is well worth a visit, as it's the most complete abbot's residence still standing in Britain.

A recently added display on the Stone of Destiny explores the history of the stone and its journey to the abbey in 1951. It had been removed from Westminster Abbey during an infamous heist.

Edzell Castle

More of a country house than a fortified structure, this castle was built in the 16th century on top of a much earlier motte and bailey timber fortification. Overlooking the Glenesk River, and founded by the Lindsay family, it stands now as a ruin. The castle has stunning red sandstone walls and a lovely parkland for exploring. Walled gardens were added in the early 17th century, though its current conformation was set in the 1930s. The nearby town (now extinct) of Edzell lives on in the name of the castle.

It is open all year, and the garden has intricate relief carvings. It is thought to have links to esoteric traditions, including Rosicrucianism and Freemasonry. Each of the carved panels (three sets of seven) represent the Cardinal Virtues (west wall), the Liberal Arts (south wall), and the Planetary Deities (east wall). There is also a bath house and summer house around the garden, and decorative topiary.

Glamis Castle/Gardens/Eassie Stone

No account of mystical places in Scotland would be complete without a mention of Glamis Castle, counted as the most beautiful and most haunted of Scotland's castles. While Shakespeare places Macbeth here in his Scottish play, the historical king had no connection to Glamis.

Crenellations and turrets abound, giving it the look of a French chateau, and the lovely red color of the stone make it stand out in the countryside. It is surrounded by formal and informal gardens and was once a religious center.

The present structure was built in the 17th century, but the Lyon family has been there since the 14th century. Before that, it had an ancient royal seat of Scottish kings. In 1034 CE, King Malcolm II was murdered at Glamis. Shakespeare writes that Duncan was also murdered there, but as I mentioned before, he played fast and loose with historical facts.

It has since been in the hands of the Bowes-Lyons family, the Queen Mother grew up at Glamis, and Princess Margaret was born there. Don't miss the crypt and the more medieval parts of the castle. There are many reported ghosts, including The Woman without a Tongue, The Grey Lady (Janet Douglas, Lady Glamis, burned as a witch in 1537), a young servant boy, Earl Beardie, (the 4th Earl of Crawford). There is even a legend of the Monster of Glamis, a deformed child born into the family, kept locked up in the tower, and bricked up after his death.

Kirriemuir, J. M. Barrie's Birthplace

Who doesn't know about Peter Pan? Explore the birthplace of the author, J. M. Barrie. The upper floors of the house are preserved to look like they would have when he was born, and next door is an exhibition of his literature and theater works. Children can dress up as some of his characters, and there is a garden with a Peter Pan Statue, as well as a gift shop.

The town itself has many buildings with a witches *stane* (a Scots word for "stone") built into the front to ward off evil. This is a hard gray stone set into the red sandstone of the region. There is a Witch Pool, a small pond outside of town, where witches were supposedly drowned. There is also a Pictish stone called the Eassie Stone in nearby Eassie. This town was thought to be a place of monastic importance at one time, as well.

Meigle Pictish Stone Museum

One of the largest collections of Pictish Carved Stones in Scotland is here in this old schoolhouse in the village of Meigle. This was possibly the home of King *Pherath*, who ruled Pictland from 839 to 842 CE.

There are many magnificent stones to see here, and three large cross-slabs dominate the display. The largest, Meigle 2, is eight feet tall. The earliest is Meigle 1, and may have originally been an ancient standing stone, as there are still prehistoric cup-and-ring marks near the base. There is now an ornate cross on the front, and a collection of Pictish symbols on the back. The stones are well-preserved and offer incredible detail and precision. It is well worth a visit for anyone interested in the ancient carvings of the Picts. The museum is only open from April to September, so plan accordingly.

Sueno's Stone

This huge stone stands at about 21 feet tall. This Pictish Carved stone is the largest surviving stone of its type in Scotland and is covered with spectacular details. It is now covered with a protective armored glass structure but can be seen clearly. It may have been moved at one point, as descriptions in the 18th century have it elsewhere. There are interwoven vine symbols along the edges, with a Celtic cross on the western face.

Acting as a stone version of the Bayeux Tapestry, a large battle scene is on the eastern face, a story told in several horizontal strips set in panels. It's dated to between circa 600-1000 CE, and there is much debate as to what the battle scene is supposed to be describing. Many guess that it is the defeat of the Picts by the Scots of Dalriada, under King Kenneth MacAlpin, circa 841. Other theories name Norse battles, such as against the Norse King Swein Forkbeard (Sueno). Legend says that Macbeth met his three witches at the stone.

Doocote

Tealing Souterrain & Doocote

This curved, stone-lined passage was once likely used for food storage in Neolithic and Iron Age times. It would have been covered by roof slabs and turf, so would have been invisible except for the small entrance. It measures twenty-seven yards in length and over six feet tall, and has interesting triangular stones set along the bottom of the wall for support.

It would have been cool and dry inside, great for storing food and keeping it fresh. It was probably built dome time circa 100 CE. It gives interesting insight into the lifestyle and needs of people during that time.

The "doocot" or dovecote, a structure built to house pigeons or doves for food, was built in 1595 by Sir David Maxwell, and is an unusual lectern shape.

Argyll and Bute

Arduaine Garden

Twenty miles south of Oban, situated on the coast, this lush and mossy garden is a delightful place. It benefits from the warm winds of the Gulf Stream and is colorful in all seasons. It has twenty acres of woodland plants, including rhododendrons, camellias, azaleas, and magnolias.

For those with a taste for the exotic, you can find Blue Tibetan poppies, Chatham Island forget-me-nots and giant Himalayan lilies. There is a cliff top panoramic view that is easily accessible, but the gardens themselves are private and give a feeling of intimacy. A large part of the park is handicapped-accessible.

Auchagallon Stone Circle

Located on the coast of the Isle of Arran, this circle commands a fantastic view across Machrie Moor and the coast of the island. It does require a short climb up from the farm track. It has not been excavated, so there is still a great deal of mystery about its purpose and extent.

It was built circa 2000 BCE and has fifteen upright slab stones around a large cairn. It is built on a sloping hill, and the downhill stones are slightly taller, so the tops are roughly even.

Bonawe Iron Furnace

If you have any interest in the industrial age, this is a great place to indulge your curiosity. The furnace, located in a beautiful setting at the head of Loch Etive. The nearby Glen Nant National Nature Reserve is the most complete charcoal-fueled ironworks in Britain.

It was founded in 1853, and the displays explain the industrial heritage and how pig iron was made. It produced up to seven hundred tons of iron per year for over one hundred years and shows a map of where the ore was extracted from in the hills surrounding the site. It was built here to bring the iron ore to where charcoal was readily available, thus nearby woodlands were needed. Up to six hundred tree cutters and charcoal burners were employed across a huge area.

Castle Stalker

Castle Stalker

If you've ever watched Monty Python and the Holy Grail, you will have seen Castle Stalker. Known as the *Castle of Aaaargh!*, it shows up near the end of the movie. While it's easy enough to see from the road, it is built on a tidal islet in Loch Laich, and therefore a bit more difficult to get to, especially at high tide.

It was originally a small fort built in 1320 by Clan MacDougall, and then owned by the Stewarts and Clan Campbell. It has since been taken back by the Stewarts, who spent ten years rebuilding and restoring it to habitability. It remains a private home but is open to the public at selected times during the summer.

Glenbarr Abbey

Home of the Clan MacAlister. Twenty miles north of the Mull of Kintyre, you can explore the heritage and home of the Clan MacAlister. They have historical records to conduct your own research, guided tours, and a chance to visit with the head of the Clan. In the winter, there is a midwinter *ceilidh*, a party held by the laird for his servants and neighbors.

The original house was built circa 1700 and may have originally been a tavern or horse-changing station for travelers. It was called Barr House at first, and then the village of Glenbarr grew around it. The current house was designed by James Gillespie Graham and completed in 1815. It was newly named Glenbarr Abbey, though it was never used as a religious house.

Glen Coe

Glen Coe itself is beautiful, with soaring mountains and serene glens, as well as the lovely desolation of the nearby Rannoch Moor. But its history leaves a haunted feeling to any visit. It is also a mystical spot, the birthplace of Oisìn, according to a local bard, John Cameron.

Glen Coe is said to mean the "Glen of Weeping," and reflects the horrible events surrounding the Glen Coe Massacre in 1692. There is an historical fiction book that recounts this horrible time, *Lady of the Glen*, by Jennifer Robeson. George R. R. Martin also used this event as an inspiration for his story of the Red Wedding, in his Game of Thrones series.

Holy Island

Just next to the Isle of Arran, this two-thirds mile by two-mile island has a long history as a sacred site. There is a holy well with healing properties, a hermit cave from St. Molaise, a 6th century monk, and evidence of a 13th century monastery. Runic writing can be found in the cave. Several areas of the island are dedicated to religion and nature. Currently, a Buddhist community is living on the island, practicing Tibetan Buddhism. A community of nuns is on the southern end of the island. There is a wildlife preserve with Eriskay ponies, Saanen goats, and Soay sheep.

Fionnphort

Iona Abbey

Whether you are here for religious reasons or not, there is no denying the rich ecclesiastical history on this island. This small island off the southwest end of the Isle of Mull was host to the first established monastery in Scotland, by St. Columba of Ireland in 563 CE, which began the conversion of Picts to Christianity, and was a leading force in Celtic Christianity. This may also have been the origin of Ireland's Book of Kells as well as the Celtic Cross as we know it today.

Samuel Johnson visited in 1773, and wrote, *"That man is little to be envied, whose patriotism would not gain force upon the plain of Marathon, or whose piety would not grow warmer among the ruins of Iona."*

The present abbey was built circa 1203 and a convent was established in 1208. There is an Iron Age hill fort dating from circa 100 BCE, several gift shops of local craftsmen, and the Infirmary Museum to explore.

The island is truly steeped with peace and tranquility. My short visit was truly memorable, despite being a rainy, overcast day, and I highly recommend it. The island can be reached via a short ferry ride from Fionnphort on Mull.

Islay

Known as the Queen of the Hebrides, this small island is Scotland's fifth largest island. There is much evidence of prehistoric settlement, with an arrowhead from 10,800 BCE discovered, and today has over three thousand inhabitants. *Dùn* Nosebridge is an Iron Age fort on a prominent crag with great views of the landscape. The odd name could come from several different mixed Scottish Gaelic and Old Norse sources, such as *knows-borg* ("fort on the crag") or knaus-bog ("turf fort"). There is also a ruined broch at *Dùn Bhoraraic*, and the remains of several roundhouses. The Kildalton High Cross dates to around 800 CE and is the last unbroken ringed Celtic cross in Scotland.

The picturesque ruins of Dunnvaig Castle, a MacDonald stronghold, sit on one coast. It has a total of eight whisky distilleries, more than enough to keep even the keenest enthusiast happy, including Laphroaig, Ardbeg, and Bowmore. Birdwatching, hill-walking, horseback riding, and fishing are popular activities, especially during the winter, when large flocks of wild geese visit. About a quarter of the population speaks Gaelic.

Isle of Arran

Described as "Scotland in miniature," this island has a bit of everything. It has been continuously inhabited since Neolithic times and was colonized from Ireland in the 6th century. St. Brendan may have founded the monastery of *Aileach* on the island, and St. Molaise is said to have been active there.

It is divided into Highland and Lowland areas by the Highland Boundary Fault and is a popular destination for geologists. Beautiful beaches, mountains, rolling hills and spectacular sea views, combined with a wealth of flora and fauna, make this a great, compact vacation spot.

There are odd sandstone structures that look like sand dunes, chalk deposits, and volcanic formations. It is ringed by post glacial raised beaches, such as King's Cave. Several standing stone groups, such as the six circles on Machrie Moor, as well as several Neolithic cairns, have been excavated, and there is evidence of humans dating back as far as eight thousand years. There are a couple of castles, such as Brodick and Lochranza, and the monastery of Aileach.

Isle of Staffa

Isle of Staffa

If the weather is good, you could catch a ferry from Mull to this lonely island, covered in puffins, kittiwakes, and other seabirds. Be prepared, though, we had to wait three days until the weather had cleared enough for us to go! The odd hexagon stone structures are something out of true legend, the same legend as the Giant's Causeway in Northern Ireland comes from. This is the other end of the Causeway, where Fingal (Finn mac Cumhaill) the giant had his cave. Mendelssohn wrote music about the place in his Hebrides Overture. The stone structure is volcanic basalt, resulting in the extraordinary pattern of columns that makes this place unique.

Inverary Castle

Who doesn't want to see a fairytale castle? Situated on the shores of Loch Fyne, this castle dates from the 1400s, but the present form was built in the 1700s, and then renovated after a fire in 1877. It is fully restored and decorated, and open for tours. Get there early, before the tour buses arrive!

The sixteen acres of gardens are well set for the different seasons, with daffodils around Easter, and rhododendrons and azaleas during the summer. Heathers, roses, and other trees fill out the rest of the year.

Kilmartin Glen

This area has a high concentration of Neolithic and Bronze Age sites, more than three hundred and fifty ancient sites in a six-mile radius. This must have been an integral part to the Ancient's life to have spent so much time creating these megalithic sites. There are standing stones, a henge, a "linear cemetery" with five burial cairns, and many cup and ring decorated stones. The royal center of the Dàl Riata at Dunadd is in the north of the glen, and there is a Museum of Ancient Culture in the village of Kilmartin.

The site includes Glebe Cairn, the Nether Largie Cairns and Standing Stones, and the Ri Cruin Cairn. The churchyard in Kilmartin has three stone crosses, the seven Poltalloch stones, and twenty-three stones in the lapidarum. Many of the carvings have predominant decorative themes such as knights and swords. Kilmartin House Museum does a fantastic job of tying in the disparate bits and presenting them in a comprehensive way.

Loch Etive

Everyone knows about Loch Ness and Loch Lomond, but these are not, by far, the only lovely lochs in Scotland. Loch Etive, long and thin on the west coast, is more like a Norwegian Fjord than a loch. It is often overlooked as the modern road doesn't pass along most of its length. Surrounded by distinctive mountains, there are good tracks on both sides for hikers. There are also cruises out of Kelly's Pier at the Bonawe Iron

Furnace. It is often possible to see deer, seals, and golden eagles, or perhaps sea eagles on a trip on the loch. Be sure to bring your binoculars for the trip!

McCaig's Tower

Often called McCaig's Folly, this structure on Battery Hill dominates the Oban skyline. John Stuart McCaig commissioned this structure as a monument to his family, as well as providing winter work for local unemployed stonemasons. He loved Roman and Greek architecture and had planned for a Coliseum like the one in Rome.

His death, however, brought an end to construction after only the outer walls were built. It now sits as a prominent tower overlooking Oban, with a circumference of over two hundred yards and two tiers of arches. It is now used as a public garden and has magnificent views of the surrounding islands.

Rothesay Castle

Located on the Isle of Bute in the best natural harbor on the island, this ruined castle, built in the 13th century, has been described as one of

153

the most remarkable in Scotland for its long history and circular plan. Built by the Stewart family, it became a royal residence after surviving several Norse attacks, thanks partly to the huge curtain wall, surrounded by a wide moat. The siege from King Hakon IV lasted three days, while the attackers tried to hack their way through the stone wall with axes. This was discouraged by the pouring of boiling pitch from above. Eventually, the Norse took the castle, but they had to withdraw immediately, due to a large Scottish fleet arriving shortly thereafter.

It was excavated in the early 19th century, and some restoration was made circa 1900, but much of what you see today dated back to its original 13th century construction. There are fine views from the top of the wall back towards the mainland.

Scottish Sea Life Sanctuary

Next to Loch Creran, this sanctuary plays host to many marine animals, from octopus to sharks. You can see rays as they swim to the surface to meet you, stand in a shoal of salmon, or attend talks and demonstrations about starfish and crabs. Children can be entertained with feeding demonstrations, interactive talks, and the seal rescue facility with a pup nursery.

St. Columba's Cave

For those interested in tracing this iconic saint's footsteps, a trip to the cave is a must. This ancient site is located at Loch Caolisport and is very remote. Along with evidence of human habitation from ten thousand years ago, there are drawings of simple crosses that are believed to date from St. Columba's first arrival to Scotland from Ireland, while he awaited permission to start a monastery on Iona.

You can see an outcropping that shows two footprints, said to be those of St. Columba himself. There are footprints carved into stone in a number of places throughout Scotland and Ireland and are usually part of ancient king-making ceremonies. There is a 13th century chapel nearby, in ruins, and a holy spring.

Ayrshire

Ardrossan Castle

What is more picturesque than a ruined castle on a ridge? This moated ruin stands above the town of Ardrossan. The site dates from the 12th century, the keep from the 15th, and has a kitchen, cellars, and a well. It was used by William Wallace, where he slaughtered an English Garrison, earning it the name "Wallace's Larder." This was Clan Barclay's keep, partially destroyed during the Wars of Scottish Independence. It was later rebuilt by Sir John Montgomery, the 7th Baron of Eaglesham, but was demolished again by Cromwell's forces. If you explore, do so with caution, as the ruins are condemned.

Culzean Castle/Souter Johnnie's Cottage

A cliff-top castle on the Ayrshire coast, this is an impressive 18th century construction with a circular saloon overlooking the sea and a grand oval staircase. Then General Eisenhower was a frequent visitor and had one apartment set aside for him. During the summer, there is access to the sea caves below the castle. It is reputed to have at least seven ghosts, including a piper and a young girl. It appeared as Lord Summerisle's home in the 1970s cult classic film, *The Wicker Man*.

Nearby is Souter Johnnie's Cottage, in the village of Kirkoswald. Robert Burns spent a summer at school here, and featured in his poem,

Tam O' Shanter. The cottage is a thatched roofed place with a workshop, complete with all the tools needed for shoemaking. The garden behind the cottage has a restored thatched alehouse.

Dean Castle

Also known as Kilmarnock Castle and Boyd Castle, the lands were originally gifted to Sir Robert Boyd, Earl of Kilmarnock, by King Robert I, aka Robert the Bruce, in 1315 for their support of the Bruce at the Battle of Bannockburn (c. 1314). The Boyds ruled over Kilmarnock for over four hundred years, and today have strong historical ties with many people and events from Scottish history: Robert the Bruce, of course; James III of Scotland whose sister married a Boyd; the Covenanters, some of whom were imprisoned here; Bonnie Prince Charlie, whose rebellion was joined by the 4th Earl of Kilmarnock; and Robert Burns who was encouraged to publish his poetry by the Earl of Glencairn who owned the Castle at that time.

The tower keep was completed around 1350 to replace a timber fortress, was built mainly for defense, with a few windows and the only door several yards above ground level and originally accessed by ladder. Today, the keep includes a museum of medieval armor (including equine), and a fully restored interior which is open to the top of the keep, including a minstrels' gallery, privy, and a ladies solar. In the basement, an oubliette (place of forgetting) was discovered.

In the 1460s, the manor was built beside the tower, and was the main residence until 1746 when a kitchen fire destroyed part of the manor. The thatch roofing on the tower was also set alight, destroying the keep. At the time of the disaster, the last Boyd to occupy the site, William Boyd, was in financial difficulties and was forced to sell the estate, which changed hands over the next hundred and forty-five years until Thomas Evelyn Scott-Ellis, 8th Lord Howard de Walden, inherited the property. He set about to restore the keep immediately, completing it in 1906.

Thomas Evelyn Scott-Ellis, A note should be added about Thomas. He was Eton educated, a landowner in his own right before the Dean inheritance, a writer of several books and plays, and patron of the arts and music. He served in the Boer War, and while rebuilding the Dean Estates, he also trained for the 1908 Olympics where he competed as a motorboat racer, and in his later years, he was President of the National Museum of Wales, and was a governor of the National Library of Wales. In 1938, he became a trustee of the Tate Gallery. He completed the manor house restoration in 1946, just months before his untimely death.

Dean Castle gets its name from "The Dean," wooded valley, which is a common place name in Scotland. The estate is surrounded by natural woodland, and today, the estate is not only fully restored, but the woodland is also home to a native wildlife restoration project, but also has a rare breed park. The full site is open to the public.

Electric Brae

Up for a wee bit of fairy magic? This is a gravity hill in Ayrshire, where cars mysteriously appear to be rolling uphill. The effect is an illusion, as the road really does go downhill. There are several of these around the world, but this stretch of road is the most well known in Scotland. *Brae* is a Scots word for hill slope or brow, and the name "electric" came when electricity was a strange new technology and applied to any odd force or phenomenon.

Robert Burns Birthplace Museum/Burns Monument/Burns Cottage

The small town of Alloway was the birthplace of Robert Burns, Scotland's greatest bard, and now houses a museum dedicated to his life, the cottage he grew up in, and a monument to his honor. In case you are worried the children will be bored, there are many interactive displays and exhibits to entertain the young, and the young at heart, as well as an outdoor play area and gardens. There is a Burns Trail of places in the area to visit. The visitor center is large and nicely displays and explains his life works.

Banffshire

Ballindalloch Castle and Gardens

The castle is known as the Pearl of the North, and dates from the 17th century. It has been the home of a single family in all that time, the Macpherson-Grants. There is a tale that the original site, on a nearby hill, was abandoned after its foundation stones had been laid. The laird had heard a voice tell him to build the fort in the cow meadow, and so he did.

Much of the décor and furniture date from the late 18th and early 19th century and are impeccably maintained. There are several ghosts said to haunt it, including that of General James Grant and The Green Lady, said to be the current laird's guardian angel. There is a rock garden, a dovecote, and is still lived in, though open to tourists during the summer months. There are workshops on its grounds as well.

Ballindalloch Whisky Distillery is here on the estate, Scotland's first Single Estate Distillery, and is well situated on the Whisky trail.

Birnie Kirk

Just south of Elgin, this small church is one of the oldest churches in continuous use in Scotland, built circa 1140, and was once a cathedral. It lost that status when a bishop died in 1184, and the county seat was moved elsewhere. The site it was built on what was believed to be the site of an earlier Celtic church, possibly dedicated to St. Brendan the Navigator. St. Brendan was thought to have traveled west from Ireland on a voyage of discovery, and possibly reached Iceland, or even Newfoundland.

Though small, the church is very well built with lovely stained-glass art, including a window dedicated to St. Columba. The square-shaped Coronach Bell is over a thousand years old and is thought to have been blessed by the Pope, though no one can say precisely which Pope. There is a Pictish stone in the kirkyard with a carving of an eagle, linking this church with the first Pictish church on the site.

Cairngorm Reindeer Centre

Fancy playing with some reindeer? Britain's only herd is found free ranging in the Cairngorm Mountains. The animals were re-introduced to Scotland in 1952 to a Swedish Reindeer Herder named Mikel Utsi. Today, there are about a hundred and fifty tame reindeer, most of them on the Glenlivet Estate. You can visit them daily during the summer months, though they are more difficult to find in the winter. Feeding or going on a trek to see the animals can be an unusual and interesting day out. The calves are born in May and June, and some of the reindeer are very friendly. Be careful, they might try to search your bags for treats!

Cairngorm Mountains

Inveravon Pictish Stones

Located within the Inveravon Parish Church to protect them from the elements, these four carved stones date back to between 600 and 800 CE. There may have been a chapel dedicated to St. Drostan on this site from the 600s. Later, a church dedicated to St. Peter was built in 1108. Nearby is a holy well dedicated for him. The current church was entirely rebuilt in 1806, which is when the four carved Pictish stones were brought inside, to protect them from the weather. The stones have carvings of an eagle, a mirror and comb, a triple disc, and other common Pictish symbols for which we have no verified interpretation.

Pluscarden Abbey

Pluscarden is the only medieval monastery in Britain still inhabited by monks and being used for its original purpose. It was founded in 1230 by King Alexander II of Scotland and lies in the peaceful Glen of the Black Burn, about six miles from Elgin. Alexander wanted to demonstrate his authority over a disputed portion of his kingdom, so he established Pluscarden, Beauly, and Ardchattan Priories.

It isn't open to the public to view, so you can only see the grounds and the main chapel. However, this does offer some lovely stained-glass windows and some carved stones. The rest of the abbey is reserved for the monks' use, and those guests on retreat. It's rather surreal to explore a working, living abbey, after seeing so many in ruins, crumbling from the weight of the years.

Speyside Cooperage

Just south of Craigellachie, this fascinating place will show you the process of creating the barrels used in the famous Speyside whisky. You can see artistic stacks of casks outside, a huge barrel bridge, café and shop, and exhibitions ("from acorn to cask") with all sorts of informative displays. You can even make your own barrel!

Berwickshire

Coldingham Priory

While this church is in some ruin, it continues to be a meeting spot for the local Church of Scotland parish for Coldingham. The grounds have a community garden with a monastic theme, growing plants with medicinal and aromatic properties. The priory is constructed of somewhat pinkish stone, which becomes especially vibrant in the rain. Two of the walls (north and east) are incredibly ornamented, while the others are strikingly plain. There is a stonework graveyard, with headstones, coffin lids, and other bits of funereal sculpture, all set aside in a strange assemblage.

There has been a monastery on this site since 635 CE and is associated with a Northumbrian princess who became St. Aebbe. Much of the church you see today was started in 1662, after several times of being destroyed and rebuilt.

Near the priory, you can find the Edrom Arch. Originally part of a Norman Church, this arch was preserved as the entrance to a mausoleum, showing off the intricate archway carvings. It was the entrance to the Church of the Virgin Mary at least from 1130. In 1732 it was moved to the mausoleum. This site is not far from Coldingham Priory above.

Mellerstain House

This Georgian house north of Kelso in the Borders was designed by William and Robert Adam and is the only remaining complete building of their design. It is well known for its beauty, with a highly decorated and embellished interior, period furniture and a fine art collection. Currently, it is home to the 13th Earl of Haddington. The art collection includes work by Gainsborough, Nasmyth, Ramsay and Van Dyck. There are Italianate terraced gardens, areas for picnics, a playground for children, and a lake to attract visitors.

Caithness

Caithness Broch Centre.

Have you explored some of the many brochs in Caithness, Orkney, Shetland or Lewis, only to wonder more about the people who lived there? Then the Caithness Broch Centre is a place to visit. There are more brochs in Caithness per square mile than anywhere else.

The center details the lifestyles and customs of the people who built and lived in the various brochs around Scotland. It's built inside an old schoolhouse on the main road from Wick to John O'Groats. A broch is a dry-stone construction tower with two circular walls. Stairways were built within the walls, and they were very popular during the last couple of centuries BCE and the first centuries CE. No one is certain if they were defensive structures, living quarters, or both.

Castle of Mey and Gardens

Formerly known as Barrogill Castle, this is the northernmost castle on the mainland of the UK and has lovely views of the Orkney Islands and the Old Man of Hoy on clear days. Though modest in size, it is in excellent condition, and decorated in a very homey way. There are gardens and an animal center, a tearoom and shop for visitors. You can even arrange to get married there. You can climb the tower within the walled garden as well.

The castle was an officers' rest home in WWII, and then purchased by Queen Elizabeth, The Queen Mother, who used it for holidays. She had seen it while mourning her husband's death and fell in love with the place.

She restored it and made it a tribute to her late husband, King George VI. Since her death, it was given to a trust and opened to the public.

Grey Cairns of Camster

Among the oldest stone monuments in Scotland, these two Homes of the Dead were built over five thousand years ago. Their location, on a windswept lonely moor, probably ensured their unusual state of preservation and survival.

The two cairns are quite different. One is a round structure, about twenty yards in diameter, while the other is seventy-six yards in diameter, strung out along a ridge line. You can stand upright even in the smaller of the two burial chambers, the Round Cairn. The Long Cairn is sixty-six yards long and twenty-two yards wide, and has two curved forecourts, one at each end. Excavations in the 1800s discovered burnt bones, pottery, tools and skeletal remains. The entrances require crawling in and are not for the claustrophobic.

Hill o' Many Stanes

Hill O' Many Stanes

While physically not incredibly impressive, such as the Ring of Brodgar, the Hill O' Many Stanes is interesting in its own right. It boasts about two hundred stones arranged in a fanned-out pattern, none more than a yard high. Believed to have been created during the Bronze Age, this windswept hill on the coast could have been set to track lunar movements, but many other similar stone row arrangements can be linked to the moon. This type of stone row construction is unknown outside Caithness and Sutherland.

Laidhay Croft Museum

Consisting of three main buildings, this museum of crofting life is on the A9 near Dunbeath, set in a 200-year-old longhouse. The long white thatched building stands out against the landscape, easily seen from the road, sparkling white when the sun shines. The site includes a barn and threshing machines to complete the picture.

The crofts are similar to the blackhouses of the Western Isles, with a central peat hearth to provide warmth and cooking fire, and a door in the front and the back. Often there was a drainage ditch through the center of the croft to carry away animal waste, especially during the long winter months, when livestock were kept inside. Usually, the uphill side of the house would be where the humans would live. You can really get a sense of the lifestyle these folk had lived from the displays.

North Coast of Scotland

So, it's not exactly hidden, but until the past few years, it's rarely mentioned. We drove all along this coast from Orkney to our turn down to Ullapool. Along the way we saw deer, sheep butts (cavorting), shaggy coos, and some of the most spectacular scenery I saw on my entire trip. There were sheer cliffs, sandy beaches, blue and aquamarine bays, diving seabirds, and rolling green hills. Each time we turned another corner, came around another bend, we would scream "Oh, this is the most beautiful thing I've ever seen!"

And then we would turn another corner, and scream it again, and again, and again. Why had no one mentioned this delightful part of Scotland to me in my research? I never came across anything talking about the incredible beauty of this drive.

I had imagined it would be a fairly boring drive across barren cliffs and dry, brown fields, but I was so very, very wrong. There were glens and valleys, mountain tarns with crystal clear reflections of the puffy clouds above. Tantalizing glimpses of the seaside peeked through mountains to the right. By the time we arrived at Ullapool, we were almost drained from the constant beauty and stunning landscapes we had driven through.

Smoo Cave

Smoo Cave

This is the largest sea cave in Scotland that was formed by both sea and river water. It is not difficult to climb down, though there are many, many steps. Some are a bit tricky, but the place is in good repair. There is normally a guided tour into the cave, but they can be canceled due to flooding, but the cave remains open. As you enter the mouth of the cave, you can see there is a cave stream coming out of the mouth of the cave; walk over the bridge, and then into the cave.

Walk into the underground waterfall cavern...oh, so powerful, so incredible! There is a hole in the cave itself that lets in some sunlight, so you can see this strong, massive waterfall pushing the water out. It's not some mountain stream trickle, but a full-blown, powerful fall. I got soaked from the spray just standing and gazing at it.

Whaligoe Steps

Whaligoe (Whale Geo or Inlet of Whales) is a small port town near the town of Wick, and primarily a harbor for fishermen. The three hundred and sixty-five man-made steps were used by the wives to haul up the creels (baskets) of herring their husbands caught. They were gutted on the harbor and taken up the steps to be sold in Wick, eight miles away.

The steps are a bit difficult to find, as they are not signposted on the main road (look for the town of Ulbster off the A99). Also, take great care in climbing or descending the steps. They're well-maintained, but they can be slippery, especially in fog or wet weather. There are spectacular sea cliffs and many sea birds, as well as a sea cave to explore.

Clackmannanshire

Alloa Tower

The Clan Erskine family, also known as the Earls of Mar, lived in this medieval tower dating from the 14th century. It is one of the earliest and largest of Scotland's tower houses, an impressive square keep. It had a larger classical house around it at one point, but now stands alone once again. There are four floors to explore, and even an abbot's curse.

The curse was placed on John Erskine, the 17th Earl of Mar by the Abbot of Cambuskenneth. The curse predicted he should rise high, but fall hard, and his work be never finished. His lands were to go to strangers, until all he held dear was in ruin. In effect, the curse was true, Mar's Wark (the townhouse Erskine was building) was never finished. The parts that are finished have an amazing display of mermaids, gargoyles and monsters on its crumbling walls. You can also see a dungeon, a stone well built into the tower walls, period costumes and art from the family's private collection.

Clackmannan Stone

This ancient stone is associated with the Celtic God of the sea, _Manau_ or _Mannan_. It rests on a larger stone next to the Mercat Cross and Tollbooth at the top of Main Street in the town of Clackmannan. The legend is that Robert the Bruce, while in town, lost his glove. He asked where it was, and was told to "look about ye," as the county coat of arms includes a pair of gloves.

Dunmore Pineapple

A folly is a structure made for no purpose other than to be pretty. They were very common in the 18th and 19th centuries, and usually found at the end of estate gardens. This one looks like a giant pineapple on a hothouse, which gives it its name, and is located in Dunmore Park, just northwest of Airth. It's said to be the most bizarre building in Scotland. There are several different architectural styles in play at Dunmore, including Palladian, Ionic columns and Tuscan columns.

The estate has a large country mansion and two large walled gardens. Walled gardens kept out the winds and allowed a sheltered environment for more delicate flowers and trees to flourish, plants that normally wouldn't survive this far north.

Dumfriesshire

Ae Totem Pole

This wooden carved pole, standing sixteen feet high, was created as part of the Ae Youth Eye project in 2006, by chainsaw sculptor, Peter Bowshor. Its entire surface is covered in carvings, many of them elements of the natural world, such as eagles, herons, deer, foxes, and owls, but also with some modern imagery as it pertains to nature. The background pine motive separates the different images.

Drumlanrig Castle & Gardens

Nicknamed the "Pink Palace" for the pink sandstone construction, Drumlanrig is located on the Queensberry Estate near Dumfries. This majestic manor house was constructed in the late 17th century as a perfect example of Renaissance architecture. The house was constructed by the first Duke of Queensberry, William Douglas and is home to the current Duke and Duchess of Buccleuch and Queensberry.

You probably won't have time to explore all the one hundred and twenty rooms, but you can see the seventeen turrets and four towers from the outside, at least. The art collection is extensive, and contains works by

Rembrandt, da Vinci, and many others. The ninety-thousand-acre estate has walks, elegant gardens, biking trails, fishing, and kids' activities.

Gretna Green

Many may have heard of Gretna Green, it is even featured in some traditional songs, and in some movies. It has become the Scottish version of Las Vegas, for quick weddings, thanks to Lord Hardwicke's Marriage Law, a strict law enacted in England in the 18th century where couples had to reach the age of 21 to marry without their parents' consent. The law didn't apply to Scotland, where couples over the age of 16 could marry with or without parental consent. This was still the case until the law was changed to 19 years old in 2022. Gretna Green is the first village over the Scottish Border, easily accessible to travelers from England bent on matrimony.

The more unusual aspect is that the most respected tradesman, the blacksmith, often performed the ceremony, and as a result, Gretna Green has a huge collection of anvils. In ancient times, the blacksmith was often considered a sorcerer or magician for his ability to change rock into useful metal. Perhaps some of that mystical reputation is still remembered in Gretna Green.

Twelve Apostles Stone Circle

Located between the villages of Hollywood and Newbridge, this is the fifth largest stone circle in Britain, and the largest on the mainland of Scotland. It has eleven stones, five of which are earth-fast. The tallest upright stone is six feet tall. The circle is almost one hundred yards in diameter, but it isn't a true circle, it's sort of flattened. Some of the stones have many cup marks on them.

Most stone circles have few artifacts found inside or buried nearby. Usually some burnt bones or pottery are all that remains of our forebears. However, a four-inch bronze figure was uncovered around 1882, a statue later identified as that of St. Norbert, and dated to the 12th century.

Ruthwell Cross

Built probably by Anglo-Saxon monks in Northumbria but was brought to Scotland. The traditional story is that it was originally sited on the Solway Firth. It is currently housed in the Ruthwell Parish Church, away from the elements. The cross stands seventeen feet tall, and the carvings are well-defined. It is probably the oldest surviving "text" of English poetry, before any known manuscripts. There are both decorative carvings and runic and Latin inscriptions on the cross. One side has a scene of Mary Magdalen drying Christ's feet, while the other has Christ as judge, with two animals. There are many other panels, and the meanings of them all are subject to debate among scholars.

While during the 16th century Reformation, the cross was left unharmed. It was eventually ordered for dismantling in 1640 by orders from the General Assembly of the Church of Scotland, citing, "*many idolatrous monuments erected and made for religious worship*" to be "*taken down, demolished, and destroyed.*"

It wasn't until 1642 that the cross was actually destroyed and scattered around the churchyard. In 1823, church minister, Henry Duncan, set about collecting all the pieces he could find, and restored the cross. He commissioned a new crossbeam, as the original was lost. He then erected it in the manse garden. The Runic symbols have been translated to, *Krist wæs on rodi. Hwepræ'l þer fusæ fearran kwomu / æþþilæ til anum.* Or in modern English as "*Christ was on the cross. Yet / the brave came there from afar / to their lord.*"

Dunbartonshire

Bearsden Roman Baths

Situated on a Roman road on the northwest edge of Glasgow, the remains of this bath house were discovered when the old Victorian houses in the area were demolished in 1973 in a plan to build apartment blocks. It is the best surviving example of a bath house in Scotland. The earliest known settlement in the area dates to 142-144 CE when the Romans occupied the region between the Antonine Wall and Hadrian's Wall. Little of the Roman Fort built here is left, but the bathhouse is well-preserved.

Glasgow Necropolis

A necropolis is a City of the Dead, and this one, built in 1832, is next to Glasgow (St. Mungo's) Cathedral. Pressure began in Britain to create pretentious cemeteries for the wealthy following the creation of Père Lachaise Cemetery in Paris. One of the oldest monuments is that of an 1825 statue of John Knox, a 16th century Scottish clergyman and leader of the Protestant Reformation, viewed as the father of the Presbyterian denomination. Other monuments include those to Scottish chemist and industrialist, Charles Tennant, who invented bleaching powder and founded an industrial dynasty; the John Henry Alexander monument, manager of the Theatre Royal; Blackie and Sons Publishing; and others, as well as war memorials, still-born children and others. In all, over fifty thousand people are memorialized or buried here in this thirty-seven-acre garden of sculpture, and each one has a story to tell.

There is no formal grid layout, and the paths meander around many of the larger monuments. Be sure to allocate plenty of time to wander the Byzantine paths and explore the fantastic funereal sculptures.

People's Palace and Winter Gardens

Located in Glasgow, this museum and glasshouse was opened in 1898 by the Earl of Rosebery. At a time when the city was one of the most overcrowded and unhealthy places to live, the palace and gardens provided a cultural retreat for the people, a place to enjoy nature and relax, even when nature isn't behaving. If the weather is inclement during your stay, it provides an excellent haven from the elements.

You can see the social history of Glasgow, telling the story of the people from 1750 to today. The Winter Gardens has exotic plants and palms to enjoy year-round. There is a café to relax in, and a recently restored Doulton Fountain outside to enjoy.

St. Mungo Museum of Religious Life and Art

This is the only public museum dedicated only to religion and is filled with stained glass and sculptures. It is not solely concentrated on Christian faith, either, as it has exhibits on Islamic Calligraphy, Sikhism, Judaism, Hinduism and a Zen garden.

The museum was constructed in 1993 on the site of a medieval castle-complex, formerly the residence of the bishops of Glasgow. It has a sort of medieval style to blend into the architectural style of its neighbor, the Provand's Lordship, Glasgow's oldest house. It's near the Necropolis, so it makes a good day trip to visit both.

Willow Tea Rooms

One of Glasgow's dearest darlings is artist and architect, Charles Rennie Mackintosh. If you fancy Art Deco, or art history, stop by for some tea at this lovely shop. Mackintosh had complete control over its décor, from windows to chairs, architecture and layout, and it remains a sweet stop from the madness that is downtown Glasgow.

Mackintosh had met Catherine Cranston, the daughter of a tea merchant and a strong supporter in the temperance movement. In order to provide a place to drink non- alcoholic beverages, Mackintosh designed this venue for people to relax and drink tea in several rooms within one building. He provided artwork and murals for several of her other tea rooms, but this one he designed completely.

Different rooms have different themes. The Ladies' Tea Room was in light colors of white, silver and rose, while the Men's Tea Room was darker, with oak paneling and gray canvas. The willow motif is an integral part of the decoration in the interior, as well as the timberwork in the furniture and building.

East Lothian

Athelstaneford

This town gets its name from a battle between the Saxon King *Aethelstane*, and his rival, Pictish King *Hungus*, in the 9th century. The legend says the Picts won the battle after they saw a white cross of clouds in the sky. Attributing their victory to Saint Andrew, they adopted his cross on the flag (which remains today), and he became their patron saint. Aethelstane was slain at the river crossing, thus the name Athelstaneford.

While the historicity of the legend is debated, it has at least lent a name to the area and the ford.

The village contains the National Flag Heritage Centre, housed in an oddly shaped doocot (dovecote) built in 1583. There is a "Saltire Trail" which has various local landmarks in the area.

Chesters Hill Fort

This fort offers us a mystery. A series of ramparts and an Iron Age fortified village which has remained unexcavated offers some mystery. An elaborate system of ramparts and ditches were created, and no one is certain why. A better site would be the higher hill next to it, but instead, this spot was chosen. By choosing the lower site, it was vulnerable from the higher ground to projectile weapons such as arrows or slings. It was later built over by a settler for whom the ramparts were less important, it seemed.

Dunbar Castle

It makes me sad to see such a frail remnant of what was once a mighty fortress. The vagaries of time, destruction and neglect rob us of so much of our history. This was once a center of power for the ancients, a spot of particular strategic importance in Scotland.

The name of this castle comes from the Brythonic language, *Dyn Barr* (fort of the point). It was already a defensive structure in the 7th century for the Kings of Bernicia. It was said to have been burned down by Kenneth MacAlpin, king of the Scots. The first stone castle on the site is thought to have been built in 1070 CE by Gospatric, Earl of Northumbria. Though it was besieged many times, it had a reputation of invulnerability.

It was in December 1567, by order of the Parliament of Scotland, following the Battle at Carberry Hill in June and a siege in September, that Dunbar and the fortress on Inchkeith were to be "*cast down utterly to the ground and destroyed in such a way that no foundation thereof be the occasion to build thereupon in time coming.*" The following year, some of those stones were used to construct the quayside on the Shore of Leith. What remains of the once mighty fortress is a picturesque ruin overlooking the harbor. Access to the ruins is not allowed.

National Museum of Flight

Tired of castles and abbeys? How about some planes? Located in one of the original wartime buildings of the Royal Air Force, East Fortune Airfield, just south of the village of East Fortune, in East Lothian, this museum is a scheduled property (of national importance), so no permanent structures may be added. The hangars, control tower, and stores all remain as a testament to the history of flight in Britain.

The collection began in 1909 when the Royal Scottish Museum acquired Percy Pilcher's Hawk glider. There are many planes on exhibit today, including a 1910 thirty- three horsepower Wright engine donated by Orville Wright. There are displays on Military Aviation, Civil Aviation, Storage and Restoration and the Concorde Experience. July usually boasts an air show, and you can take helicopter flights as well. This museum has grown to become one of the most important aviation museums in the whole of Great Britain.

Preston Mill and Phantassie Doocot

The mill is an architectural oddity, with a conical roof of pantiles (S-shaped fired tiles) and is East Lothian's last working water mill. A working mill has been on this site since the 16th century, and in operation until the mid-1950s, mainly producing oatmeal. The site consists of the mill, kiln, and miller's house.

A short walk across the river, you will find the beehive shaped Phantassie boxes. The parapet is in the unusual shape of a horseshoe. There is a walled garden dedicated to the rearing of Gloucester and Berkshire pigs, Black Rock hens, and organic produce.

Tantallon Castle

If you want to explore a ruin with all sorts of interesting places, this castle has a curtain wall, inner and outer courtyards, corner turrets, portcullis, drawbridge, spiral stairs, gun-ports, garderobes, and a pit prison, Tantallon is a good place to do that. Situated on a sea cliff, it is protected on only one side by the massive curtain wall. The other three sides are protected by the sea. The castle was built in the 14th century by William Douglas, 1st Earl of Douglas, and was built to impress. There is even a resident ghost to visit, it is said to be haunted by a "courtly figure dressed in a ruff."

Fife

Balbirnie Stone Circle

While Balbirnie House is now converted into a hotel, the park is still intact for exploration, though most of that is now a golf course. Part of the park was also mined for coal at one point. The real feature is the stone circle, dating to before 2000 BCE.

There are eight stones in a partial circle, as well as some gaps where stones may have been removed. Some of the stones have cup marks and rings carved into them. No one is certain what these markings mean, or who made them, but they are common in Scottish megalithic structures. The center of the circle has a rough, square flat area with low kerb stones, and filled in with flat paving stones. Nearby are a couple of cists, or burial plots, lined with stones. Excavations took place in the 1880s and again in the 1970s, where a number of items were recovered, including an intact food container, a flint knife, and glass beads and buttons.

Isle of Harris

Burntisland Church

This is a very unusual church, built in a square plan, the nave surrounded by four aisles. The structure is supported by four huge stone columns, one at each corner. There is an ornate Magistrate's Pew, which was created in 1606, and the church has many references to the sea, anchors, ships, and other nautical emblems. The east gallery is called the Sailor's Loft and had a separate entrance and external stairs. This allowed sailors, who had to catch the tide, to leave the church quietly. This is also the church in which the commission to create a new translation of the Bible was made by James VI of Scotland, later to become James I of England. That became the "Authorized Version," or better known today as the King James Bible, giving the church its nickname, Church of the Bible.

Culross Palace and Abbey

As you pass the rather industrial outskirts of Culross town, you may not realize what a treat you are in for. Culross is like a time capsule to the 16th century, and is used for a lot of filming. The National Trust of Scotland has done a lot of work making this town frozen in time. There is an extensive hanging herb garden, the remains of the abbey, a 1626 Town House, and the narrow wynds (narrow lanes) which run through the streets. The palace itself dates from 1597 and is restored to its mustard yellow color.

The village itself was formed due to religion, coal mining and salt. It was thought to be the birthplace of Saint Mungo, and thus an abbey was formed in 1217. Though it has fallen to decay, the abbey church still works as the parish church. The heat from the coal helped the salt industry and the profits from the salt helped to build the Palace.

Falkland and Falkland Palace

In 1970, Falkland was made into Scotland's first conservation area, and it maintains its nostalgic charm as a result. Cobbled wynds and charming shops are at every turn in the village, while the Palace looms in the south.

Besides the town itself, Falkland Palace is a striking gatehouse with two towers, with a lovely parish church near the town center. There has been a structure in this spot since at least the 1300s when Robert Stewart, Duke of Albany made his home there.

There are several highlights to see in the palace, including the paneled keeper's quarters east of the gatehouse, the King's and Queen's Rooms, the Old Library and the Bakenhouse. The Chapel Royal is exquisite, with detailed decorations on the ceiling and a Tapestry Corridor nearby that is not to be missed. Extensive gardens, water-lily ponds, glasshouses and Britain's oldest tennis court complete the visit.

Secret Nuclear Bunker

This is a great place to visit in poor weather and can keep the kids entertained. The irony is all the signs pointing at "Scotland's Secret Bunker." Located in Anstruther, there is a long, sloping tunnel leading down into the paranoid world of the Cold War. It was built in the 1950s for government officials in case of emergency. There is a cold, creepy feeling inside, as if you can hear the ghosts of those who had inhabited it during that time. It has dormitories, a Royal Air Force control room, and a telephone switchboard with twenty-eight hundred outside lines. There is also a BBC Sound Studio for broadcasting from within.

Isle of Skye

Inverness-shire

Isle of Harris
The Golden Road

This road is located north of Rodel on the way to Tarbert, on the south end of Harris. It was named the Golden Road due to how much it cost to build in 1897. It's NOT for the faint of heart. Much of the ten-mile road is single lane, winding and twisting across a seemingly barren landscape, with no shoulder or leeway for any mistakes. This road runs through South Harris in an area called the Bays, traveling through the coastal townships of Lingerbay (*Lingreabhagh*), Finsbay (*Fionnsbhagh*), Ardvay (*Àird Mhighe*), Flodabay (*Fleòideabhagh*), Manish (*Mànais*), Geocrab (*Geòcrab*), and Lickisto (*Liceasto*).

Luskentyre Beach

On the southwest tip of the Isle of Harris is the wonderful Luskentyre Beach. Even with a dark, overcast sky, the waters are a bright aquamarine, and the sand is creamy white, and pristine, fine, and smooth. This beach looks like a postcard out of some Caribbean vacation spot, so out of place on this northern, rainy, windswept location. The bay is like a shining jewel set in pale, blond gold.

Isle of Skye

Armadale Castle Gardens

This impressive country house, part of the Clan Donald, stands in ruins on the south end of the Isle of Skye. It was built circa 1790 and was partly destroyed in a fire. It was rebuilt in 1815 in the Scottish baronial style "mock-Gothic." Don't miss the impressive ivy-covered main entrance to the Gothic Wing, or the Imperial Staircase. The forty acres of formal gardens are well–maintained and include the rockery and ornamental ponds.

The Museum of the Isles is part of the Clan Donald Centre. It looks a bit forbidding but has a wealth of information inside. It is located just three-quarters of a mile from the Mallaig Ferry Terminal. There's also a restaurant and gift shop on the property.

Clach Ard

It is rare to find a Pictish symbol stone on the Isle of Skye. Of the two hundred and forty-two Pictish stones in Scotland, they are mostly on the eastern side of the country. This one is near the town of Tote, about five miles northwest of Portree. *Clach Ard* means Tall Stone in Gaelic, and it's about five feet in height. It was discovered as a door jam in a nearby cottage when they were demolishing it. No one is sure what the symbols on the stone mean, though some have suggested they are dynastic symbols.

Colbost Croft Museum

This traditional croft cottage depicts island life in the 19th century. It has an open hearth in the center of the floor for a peat fire, and has two main rooms, a kitchen/sitting room, and a bedroom. There is a bare earth floor and unadorned dry-stone walls. The amenities are very basic but would have kept the family snug during the worst Skye winter, especially with the livestock in the cottage with them! There are outbuildings as well; one for storage and one for an illicit still, also good for keeping the family snug during the winter! Just next door is the Three Chimneys Restaurant.

Duirinish Peninsula

While Skye is a frequently visited part of Scotland, with good reason, few tourists make it out to Duirinish Peninsula in the northwest. It has some interesting geological features, such as the flat-topped mountains of Healabhal Mhòr, known as MacLeod's Tables. Off the west coast are three sea stacks, *An Dubh Sgeir*, *An Stac* and MacLeod's Maidens. If you're visiting the Colbost Croft Museum, it would be worth your time to see this peninsula. Dunvegan Castle, home of the Clan MacLeod, lies just inside the east shore of the peninsula, and has fantastically extensive gardens.

Dun Beag Broch

Located on the west coast of Skye, at Bracadale, this broch stands on a hillside with great views over Loch Bracadale. The broch rises to about fourteen yards and is a well-preserved structure.

Be careful when climbing, though; parts are steep and covered in grass, which will be slippery, especially on damp days. The steps and stonework are impressive, especially considering it was likely built about two thousand years ago.

It does tax the imagination a bit to picture what life was like in these brochs, and indeed, it they may simply have been used in times requiring fortifications. But brochs dot the countryside all over the north of Scotland. Originally, this one was probably about eleven yards higher than it is today and roofed with wood and thatch.

Duntulm Castle

Little more than a rambling ruin today, this precariously perched 14th-century castle was once a mighty fortification on the north tip of the Isle of Skye. Its original name was *Dun Dhaibhidh*, or David's Fort, and was built at a time when the ruling MacDonalds were feuding with the MacLeods.

By the 16th century, castle defenses had been improved, but by the 17th century, the MacDonalds had taken possession of the castle. Within a hundred years, though, the castle was abandoned when Sir Alexander MacDonald built a modern home, Monkstadt House, and used stones from the castle in the process.

In its day, this location, perched on the edge of rolling hills, was an incredibly defensible spot. Follow the paths through the bits of stone wall with care and stay within its confines for your safety. In the rain, the stones will be slick; combine this with sheep droppings, and you get very difficult footing.

At the entrance to the site, there is a cairn. It commemorates the MacArthurs, traditional pipers to the MacDonald Clan.

Dunvegan Castle

Dunvegan Castle has been the home to the MacLeod Clan for at least eight hundred years and is an imposing stronghold on the Isle of Skye. It is impressive even today, with extensive renovations inside and both formal and rambling wild gardens outside. The buildings in the castle itself have been built during ten distinct periods, beginning with the Norse Leod Olafson, born around 1200. It is likely there was a previous fortification on the headland, perhaps back to Iron Age times. The only entrance to the first castle was via the still-existing Sea Gate.

A mystical legend says that an artifact on display, the Fairy Flag, was once the shawl of a fairy woman. She was the wife of one of the MacLeod Clan who lived at the castle, and the flag is said to have magical properties. To fly the flag was to win the battle being fought, and it could be used three times. It has supposedly been used twice, successfully.

While the flag on display is little more than scraps of silk, you can use your imagination to think of what it could have been in the fairy realm.

As lovely as the castle was, the gardens were fantastic. They were wild and wandering, filled with flowers and foliage, bamboo and butterflies. We walked up to the waterfall, to the walled garden, and all around the pathways. The sheer variety and beauty of the flowers was almost overwhelming. We even saw a bright colony of mushrooms growing in the knot of a tree, protected from vandals by some mesh screen (sad, isn't it?). I felt like Alice in Wonderland, seeing plants I'd never seen before. I expected a caterpillar to be around every bend, smoking his hookah.

Dunvegan Castle

The Fairy Glen

Just behind the Uig Hotel, which is on the south edge of Uig Village, there is a small road that will take you to the glen. And yes, it is a very small and winding road, but you will get there.

The Fairy Glen is an area you really have to see to believe. Covering over three- and-a-half acres, it is strange and alien, with conical hills, rambling trees with exposed roots, and a rocky outcropping known as Castle Ewan. And it is green, simply everywhere. There is a small circle of stones laid out in a spiral, and legend says wishes are granted to girls who dance naked among them! There is narrow path up the hill; be sure to go all the way up to enjoy the view. And don't miss the disappearing stream which flows through this little valley and disappears into the hillside.

The Fairy Glen

The Fairy Pools

Located in Glen Brittle, the Fairy Pools are a short walk from the nearby parking lot (near the Sligachan Hotel) and are several aqua-blue pools. There are several waterfalls, an underwater arch in the river, and a well-made path along the left of the stream. Many pictures on the internet are mislabeled (one famously with purple flowers along aqua pools, which is really from New Zealand) so make sure you know what you are really looking for!

Giant Angus MacAskill Museum

The real Angus MacAskill was 7'9" tall and weighed five hundred pounds. He was listed in the Guinness Book of World Records as the tallest natural giant in the world until at least the 1980s. He was a member of P.T. Barnum's famous circus and could lift three hundred-and-fifty-pound barrels under each arm without effort.

He was forced to move with his family to Cape Breton, Canada, where he grew tall and strong, and many stories of his strength have risen around his legend. After his work in the circus, he retired a wealthy man, but died soon after. Though MacAskill never lived on Skye, this thatched home museum was created in his memory by a relative.

Kilmuir Graveyard & Easter Church

This graveyard is like an all-star graveyard. The pride of place belongs to the grave of Flora MacDonald, the woman who smuggled Bonnie Prince Charlie out of Scotland dressed as her Ladies' Maid. Known as "Preserver of Prince Charles Edward Stuart," she's said to have been buried in a shroud made from a bedsheet belonging to and slept in by Bonnie Prince Charlie himself. At her burial in 1790, some three thousand mourners are said to have attended, and consumed over three hundred gallons of whisky. Songs and tales have sprung up about this apocryphal tale, but no-one knows the truth of it.

Other notables include:

- **Fashion designer Alexander McQueen.** His grave marker was purposefully designed and placed to look like an ancient monument.
- **Dr. John MacLean.** This is a large burial enclosure with the inscription: "*Sacred to the memory of Johannis MacLean who being as distinguished in medicine as he was loved for his high principle pleasant manner and sound judgement died lamented by all on 1 May 1793 aged 85.*"
- **Angus Martin.** In Scots Gaelic, *Aonghas na Geoithe … Angus of the Wind*. He earned this nickname because he was known to go to sea no matter the weather. His grave slab is carved with his full effigy.
- **Charles MacArthur.** The last hereditary piper of the MacDonald clan of Duntulm Castle. His grave slab bares an incomplete inscription: "*Here lie the remains of Charles MacKarter whose fame as an honest man and remarkable piper will survive this generation for his manners were easy and regular as his music and the melody of his fingers will …*" It's said that Charles' son had commissioned the marker, but when he was drowned at sea, the stonemason figured he'd never be paid so never completed the work.

The place has a commanding view across the Minch to Harris and North Uist. Parts of the Easter church date back to the 1100s, but most is from the 1798 rebuilding.

Kilt Rock

Kilt Rock and Waterfall

Kilt Rock is beautiful and made more so when the sun is hitting it. This is an easy one to get to, as there is a large parking lot just off the main road on the Trotternish Peninsula, and a huge observation deck to see the rock and top of the waterfall beside Loch Mealt. The steel safety railings are hollow, and either by design or by accident, there are no caps on the ends of the railings. This means that, when the wind blows in the right direction, an eerie wailing can be heard, voices of the fae from the other side of the veil. The fall is the result of overflow from Loch Mealt into the sea.

Knock Castle

This 15th century castle on the east coast of Sleat on Skye is in ruins. Built by the MacLeods and captured by the MacDonalds, it is reportedly haunted by The Green Lady, a *gruagach,* a ghost who is associated with the fortunes of the family who occupies the castle. If good news is to come, the ghost will appear happy. However, if bad news is to come, she will be weeping. The castle is also said to have a *glaistig,* a spirit who cares for livestock. In order to see the castle, you must park and walk along a narrow minor trail, past a farm building. You will pass what is thought to have been a blacksmith's forge. Use caution, as the site is not maintained and can be slippery in the rain.

Lighthouse at Aird of Sleat

While it is a bit of a trek to make it to this southernmost point of the Isle of Skye, the views are well worth the effort. There is a single-track road to the small village of Aird, and the lighthouse itself is not high up. But from this vantage point, you can see the islands of Eigg and Rum, the Ardnamurchan Peninsula, and the Silver Sands of Morar. While the highest point of the area (nine hundred feet) is inaccessible, you will still see delightful visions along the road. There isn't much in the way of visitor attractions here, but the old Aird Church has been converted into a small art gallery. Check the weather before making the journey, as the views will be limited with cloud cover or rain, but if you've a sunny day to explore, it's well worth it.

The Old Man of Storr

This pointy rock outcropping is the result of ancient landslips. The area is dramatic and well worth a trek up the forest path. While you may feel like you are traveling back in time through this primeval wood, you will eventually emerge at the top of the hills and, if the mist parts, you will see the unusual rock formations of this spectacular sight.

There are three stages to this walk, but don't worry, the path is well marked. Once you park your car, head through the gate and follow the path curving up the hill. And yes, it will likely be mud, as the mists rarely leave the forest. The second stage is once you clear the forest and have a gravel path to follow. Go through a gate and up the slope to another path. It will get rough and rocky here, so take plenty of breaks. When the path splits, take the left branch. The third stage is after the split. There are some rough steps, and the "Old Man" will be on your far-right side. The path continues to turn right and face the Old Man.

Shilasdair Dye and Yarn Shop and SkySkyns

These two shops, located not far from the ruined Trumpan Church, are lovely little cottage industries (literally) run by locals. The Dye and Yarn shop has both raw materials and finished wool and yarn to purchase, and she uses mostly local flora and materials for her dye lots. She will take you on a short tour of her workshop to see the various processes. Shilasdair sells yarns internationally in local yarn shops all over the world.

The Skye Skyns leather tannery nearby also has a workshop tour, and the shop is in the loft of the great barn, with all sorts of colors and textures.

Skye Serpentarium

Founded in 1991 in Broadford, this exhibition and educational center has become a haven for unwanted and illegally imported reptiles. They have helped over six hundred creatures, and more than fifty are on display in the Serpentarium, from White's Tree Frogs to Green Iguanas.

Staffin Beach

This black rock volcanic beach isn't just black, it's green and gold, black and gray, brown, and purple. The colors of the seaweed, lichen, and rock combine for an oil painting rainbow. However, do be warned, the single-track road to get down there has very little by way of shoulder if someone is coming the other way. Check the track before you start! From the level of the beach, you can see up into the Quiraing. There are spectacular rock formations in that area, such as the Prison, the Needle and the Table. The best part is you can see real dinosaur footprints along the beach, dating from one hundred and sixty-five million years ago!

Trumpan Church

On the Waternish peninsula of Skye, this ruined church overlooks the sea. It was originally known as *Cille Chonain*, or St. Conan's Church, and probably dates from the 1300s. A striking grave marker at the east end has the carving of a claymore surrounded by plants and animals. A nearby cave was the scene of a massacre of almost four hundred of the MacDonalds by their rivals, the MacLeods. Revenge came quickly, while the MacLeods were in church at Trumpan, and set the church ablaze. The only MacLeod to escape the fire was a young girl who squeezed through a window. The church has been a ruin ever since.

Other Isles

Calum's Road

This very hidden place is simply a road, built by determination and simple tools. Malcolm MacLeod (*Calum* in Gaelic) was a crofter who lived on the north end of the Island of Raasay, near Skye. Many others also lived on the north end of the island and had to either walk several miles from where the road ended to their houses or take a ferry from Portree. Calum worked at the Rona Lighthouse and was a postman, and he campaigned for the access path to be made into a road. He was denied, so in the mid- 1960s, he decided to build the road himself, using a shovel, pick, a wheelbarrow, and a book on road making. Of course, the irony was that he never drove south, because he never got a driver's license. Capercaillie wrote a song in his honor on their album, *The Blood is Strong*, and a book of his story came out in 2006.

Cille Bharra

Also known as Kilbarr Church This collection of structures includes a medieval church and two chapels, all set within the Eoligarry burial grounds. The original church dates from the 1100s and might have had an earlier chapel dating back to the 600s, and is dedicated to St. Finbarr of Cork, Ireland. The Killbar Stone has some complex Christian-Nordic runic carvings on it and the relief of a cross, and probably dates from the 900s. The original cross is in the National Museum of Scotland, but a replica is available at Cille Bharra. Among the graves is that of Sir Compton MacKenzie, author of *Whisky Galore* and *Monarch of the Glen*. There are also some magnificent views of sandy beaches from the church.

<u>Mainland Inverness-shire</u>

Ardverikie Estate

This magnificent turreted Highland estate was the setting of the show *Monarch of the Glen*. It is set within a magnificent glen, on a promontory overlooking King Fergus's Island. The three-mile driveway winds past a huge inland beach and around the loch. While the main house remains a private home, the small gatehouse (also featured in Monarch) is available as a self-catering rental. And the estate is host to many activities, such as deer stalking, golf, fishing, and water sports, as well as hiking, birdwatching, and scenic spots for photography.

Beauly Priory

This ruined priory was a Valliscaulian monastery, established in 1230, possibly founded by Alexander II of Scotland, and supported itself by making salt. The order was eventually absorbed by the Cistercians in the 18th century. This priory houses some magnificent funereal sculpture, such as the monument to Prior Alexander Mackenzie (d. 1479) and Kenneth Mackenzie of Kintail (d. 1492), Highland chief and head of the clan MacKenzie, and nicknamed Coinneach a'bhlair or *Kenneth of the Battle*. Beauly comes from the French name, *Beau Lieu*, or Beautiful Place. It is mentioned in John Keats poem, *On Some Skulls in Beauley Abbey, near Inverness*. You may find the priory locked. If so, there should be a sign telling you where to find the key, usually at the Priory Hotel in Beauly town.

Glenfinnan Viaduct

Caledonian Canal

Built in the 19th century as a way to being much-needed work into the Highlands after the Highland Clearances, this great canal that runs for sixty miles along the Great Glen and bisects Scotland from Fort William to Inverness. There are twenty-nine working locks along the route, as well as several large lochs (don't get confused!). Anyone with an interest in engineering or transportation will be fascinated by the mechanics of the system, first built in the early 19th century. You can sail through the canal or enjoy the view at Neptune's Staircase, a ladder of eight locks that raises vessels to a height of seventy feet above sea level. This is also a great place to see Ben Nevis on a clear day.

Carved Stones of Kiel

If you have a love for carved stone, this is a must-see for you. Originally called *Cille Choluimchille*, or The Church of St. Columba of the Church, the Kiel Church was built on a site that was believed to be the site where St. Columba first settled on a high promontory, overlooking the Sound of Mull and Loch Aline. The building itself was built in the 19th century and is very attractive with red stone and white harled walls. However, the stones it houses are the most interesting feature. Some date from the 700s, others are from the 14th or 16th centuries. There are various styles, from relatively simple to highly complex.

Images of traditional west Highland ships, called *Birlinns*, adorn two of the stones. Some stones have been recarved, the original carvings under the newer ones.

You will find some skull-and-bones carvings, these are not indications of pirates, but a reminder in an illiterate age that death comes to us all.

Corrimony Cairn

About eight miles from Drumnadrochit, this cairn is unusually well preserved, with eleven standing stones and a corbeled roof. It is accessible via a footbridge over a small stream. The cairn itself is about sixty feet in diameter and is well defined. There is a circular chamber in the center, reached via a low passage, which requires crawling to enter. There are a number of cup marks in the capstone, which lies to one side. It is believed that this site dates to about four thousand years ago and may have been the burial place of a high-status woman, assumed by a bone pin found during excavation.

Glenfinnan Monument and Aqueduct

At the head of Loch Shiel, this place would be worth a visit just for the beauty. However, if you are interested either in Jacobite history or Harry Potter, there are other reasons to visit. Glenfinnan Monument was built to commemorate the place Bonnie Prince Charlie first raised his standard in 1745 to start the Jacobite Rising of that year, which ended horribly in Culloden in 1746.

The Viaduct behind it has been featured in each of the Harry Potter films as part of the Hogwarts Express route, and is made up of twenty-one arches, up to one hundred feet high. When it was first proposed, it was feared to be a monstrosity, an ugly clunking thing that would rob the area of its charm and beauty. Few would agree now, however, as it lends grace and nostalgia to the surrounding countryside.

Just west of the viaduct is Glenfinnan Station, converted into a railway museum.

You can explore a sleeping car and a dining car, complete with a verandah overlooking the valley.

Highland Wildlife Park

Opened in 1972, this is a two-hundred-and-sixty-acre safari-style park, where you can see native species of the Highlands. Visitors can see wolves, elk, yak, Pallas cats, vicuna, cranes, snow and great gray owls, and musk ox, as well as deer, reindeer, and red pandas. Recently some exotic, endangered species have been added to the animals on offer, to the tune of much controversy. It is open every day of the year, weather permitting, so it's a great option if you have restless children tired of more castles or abbeys.

Rogie Falls

We came across this place by accident on our first trip to Scotland. Just past Strathpeffer, there is a wonderful forest walk and this odd waterfall where all the rocks are diagonal. It almost makes you feel as if you have vertigo, because you know you are standing straight, but everything else seems askew. In reality, this geological formation is due to plate tectonics. The forest itself is delightfully green and verdant, and there is a small bridge over the falls where you can continue the forest path on the opposite side.

The small bridge and waterfall are a half mile down from the parking lot, and not a very difficult walk.

Silver Sands of Morar

While the road to the Silver Sands is memorable for its twists, turns, and stretches of single track, the incredible and remarkable part is the Silver Sands Beach. This white sandy beach offers sublime views across to the islands of Rum and Eigg, as well as Skye. There are a number of places to park and explore the beaches and islets along the area.

We truly felt as if we could be somewhere in the Caribbean islands with this lovely fine, white sand. The film *Local Hero* was shot near here. Sand dunes and sailboats can make for a relaxing afternoon picnic!

Treasures of the Earth

Are the children clamoring for something cool to do? Four miles from Corpach in the west Highlands, this museum holds Europe's best collection of crystals, gemstones, and fossils. It is housed in simulated caverns, with crystals over a yard tall and geodes over seven feet tall. You can see the largest gold nugget ever discovered and the history of the Scottish Gold Rush, amethyst geodes that reach seven feet tall, and sparkling gemstones at every turn. Fossils from a billion years ago and petrified amber vie with the life-sized T-Rex skull for attention.

Kincardineshire

Dunnottar Castle

In Scots Gaelic, *Dùn Fhoithear*, "fort on the shelving slope." St Ninian is said to have founded a church here in the 5th century, but it's unclear when the first fortified castle was built on this site. The earliest written reference to any fortification is found in the Annals of Ulster.

The site had been the focus of attack through the centuries, including a siege in 681 and 694, as well as a battle between King Donald II and the Vikings in 900. It's believed that King Aethelstan targeted the fort in 934. It was fought over between Edward I and William Wallace, who burned down the church and the entire English garrison within. It was the last holdout for Charles II against Cromwell in 1652 and was the hiding place for the *Honours of Scotland*, the Crown Jewels. Dunnottar was eventually forfeited to the crown and dismantled in the 1720s after coming into the possession of the Earl Marischal.

Words cannot describe this impressive castle on its cliff over the sea. It is practically the definition of the word "impregnable." Do be prepared for a long, uphill half-mile walk, though, but it is well worth the long hike. There is a second entrance for the more intrepid explorers, from the rocky creek and cave on the north side, with a steep path up the cliff. The medieval fortress dates from about the 15th century and played a prominent role through much of Scottish history. The castle is spread over three–and-a-half acres and has only a narrow strip of land to connect it to the mainland.

Fetteresso Castle

This is a 14th century tower house built in the Scottish Gothic style by the Earls Marischal of Dunnottar, though there is evidence of prehistoric use of the site, as well as medieval. There is a cursus (a series of parallel lengths of banks with external ditches which were originally thought to be early Roman athletic courses, though this is unproven, the Latin name cursus, means "course"). The most ancient part of the site includes a Bronze Age cairn with human remains inside. This was also a Bronze Age site called Malcom's Mount; legend says Malcolm I was buried here, as he was slain in Fetterosso in 954 CE.

More legends recount Jean Hunter, a woman that lived in the castle in 1659. She was accused of witchcraft and hanged at her own home. The castle is just west of Stonehaven, and therefore easily visited in conjunction with Dunnottar, listed above.

Nine Stanes Stone Circle

At this site, you get three for one! There are three stone circles in this small area, just southwest of Banchory. Two of the circles, known as Elsie the Greater and Elsie the Lesser, are within sight of each other, standing just a half a mile apart. The third site, Nine Stanes, forms a rough triangle in location, but is blocked from view by a stand of trees. The sites are very much reclaimed by nature; the stones are covered in lichen, the forest is close, one of the horizontal stones is now fallen, but this is still a must see for stone circle enthusiasts.

Kinross-shire

Loch Leven Castle

An important part of Scotland's history for over three hundred years, this castle was probably best known as the prison of Mary Queen of Scots during 1567-1568. It was here that she was forced by the powerful Scottish barons to abdicate her throne in favor of her son, James VI, still an infant. In order to reach the castle, you take a ferry across the loch to the island castle. Within the curtain wall of the castle, there is a very early tower house from the 1300s, with wonderful, vaulted ceilings still intact for the kitchens.

The present castle dates to about the 1300s and may have been built by Edward I. Certainly the English troops were there when it was captured by William Wallace in the dead of night. The "modern" incarnation likely replaced an earlier Pictish fort, from about 490 CE.

Loch Leven Heritage Trail

This walking trail runs over seven miles around the north side of Loch Leven, Scotland's largest lowland loch. It runs between Kinross Pier and Vane Farm, and has access for walkers, cyclers, and wheelchairs. The loch is a nature reserve for rare plants, insects, and birds.

Kirkcudbrightshire

Cairnholy: I & II Cairns

These two Neolithic burial cairns are remarkably complete and are situated on a hill with lovely views over Wigtown Bay. They are both open to the sky, their coverings stolen long ago. The first cairn is between four and six thousand years old and has gone through several incarnations. The excavations revealed unusual interiors, including what is believed to be the tomb of *Galdus*, a mythical Scottish King. Some of the artifacts discovered were from far away, such as a fragment from a jadeite axe from the Alps, as well as shards of Neolithic pottery, a leaf-shaped arrowhead, Peterborough- ware and Beaker-ware pottery shards, and a flint knife.

It is a bit of a hike from the parking lot, so come prepared. The sign only mentions the one cairn, but search for the second one, which is out of sight. It is well worth a visit! Go through the gate at the north end of the first cairn to access the track to the second one. The balancing slab is massive and almost perfectly flat.

MacLellan's Castle

Built in 1582 by the MacLellan family, this once the grandest house now stands in ruin; it's square and solid, imposing against the skyline, a testament to family ruin and poor decisions. It was partially built with the stones from the ruined Convent of Greyfriars nearby, as well as the stones from the old royal castle in Kirkcudbright. Perhaps this "cannibalism" doomed his home to ruin in the future?

By all accounts, Sir Thomas MacLellan was not above bending the law to his own designs, which led to his failure, when the cost of troops to keep his Irish lands grew too high. He ended up as a glover working in Edinburgh, while other branches of the family retained ownership of the castle. It's now in the care of Historic Scotland. The castle never saw hostile action or generations of remodeling, so it stands as it had after it was, in turn, "cannibalized" by other builders.

Sanquhar Castle

While it isn't easy to find, it is a fascinating place once you do. Do take care, as this ruin is still crumbling. It was built by the Crichton family circa 1400 who sold it in the mid-17th century to Sir William Douglas, 1st Duke of Queensberry who eventually sold it in 1895 to John Crichton-Stuart, 3rd Marquess of Bute, who wished to restore his ancestral home, following successful restorations at Cardiff Castle and Castell Coch in Wales. This was undertaken by arts and crafts architect and landscape designer, Robert Weir Schultz. The squarer and more structurally sound sections rebuilt of that time can still be clearly identified. Work ended following the Marquess' death in 1900.

What remains is a mix of restoration and original stonework, but still very far from completion. There are some odd noises when the wind blows through, possibly the ghost of Marion of Dalpeddar, also known as The White Lady, a girl who disappeared in 1590, supposedly murdered. A young skeleton was found in 1895, assumed to be that of Marion.

Sweetheart Abbey

Named after the embalmed heart of John de Balliol, this abbey was established circa 1100 CE for the Cistercians, known as the White Monks for their white habits. Lady Dervorguilla signed the charter, and loved her husband so much, she had his heart embalmed and placed in an ivory box with enameled silver trimmings. She was buried with her husband's heart box next to her in the sanctuary of the church.

It is situated in a lovely valley near the village of New Abbey. The abbey itself is built in deep red sandstone, and was a daughter house to Dundrennan Abbey, thus became known as the New Abbey. If you are lucky enough to visit during a sunny day, the red of the sandstone can be quite stunning.

Lanarkshire

St. Bride's Church, Douglas

This church is also known as Old St. Bride's Church, to distinguish it from the current parish church, also known as St. Bride's. Associated with the Black Douglas family, there's been a church on this site since the early 1300s, and some of the graves and mausoleums reflect that. There is one to the 7th Earl of Douglas in 1443 CE, and one to Sir James Douglas in 1330 CE, who took Robert the Bruce's heart on Crusade.

You can gain access inside if the key holder is available (there is a sign to tell you where). Inside, there is a clock thought to have been built in the 1560s, a gift from Mary, Queen of Scots, which may be the oldest working clock in Scotland. It chimes three minutes early, in honor of the Douglas family motto of "never behind."

Wanlockhead

Care to visit the highest village in the UK, and the highest pub in Scotland? Come to Wanlockhead, at an elevation of more than fifteen hundred feet above sea level, was founded in 1680 by the Duke of Buccleuch, who built a smelting plant and cottages for the workers. Wanlockhead is at the head of the Mennock Pass, part of the Southern Uplands, now boasts a lead mining museum, a walking trail, an old village smithy, and the highest pub in Scotland, the Wanlockhead Inn. The name comes from the Gaelic *Cuingealach*, or "narrow place." There are gold and lead deposits in the hills, exploited since Roman times. The Regalia of the Scottish Crown used some of the gold mined here, which tested as some of the purest gold in the world.

World of Wings

Would you like to learn how to fly a falcon, owl, or hawk? Located within the Cumbernauld Outdoor Activity Centre in North Lanarkshire, the World of Wings has the largest collection of birds of prey in Scotland. They are involved in conservation and breeding projects, as well as providing falconry courses and educational talks. The Outdoor Activity Centre also offers paint-balling, archery and off-road driving.

Midlothian

Camera Obscura: Edinburgh

Welcome to the land of illusion! Edinburgh's oldest visitor attraction since 1835, this exhibit explores the different ways in which mirrors, photography, and visual illusion can trick the eye and the mind. There is a Vortex Tunnel, a Mirror Maze, kaleidoscopes, holograms, the Ames Room, and the Camera Obscura itself, which I particularly enjoyed, as an artist. The rooftop view is amazing, and it has high-powered telescopes and binoculars to use. Explore six floors of hands-on, interactive exhibits, a great indoor alternative on a rainy day in Edinburgh.

Doon Hill Settlement

While this site is of great archeological importance, being one of the few settlements in southeast Scotland from the Anglo-Saxon Northumbrians of the 6th and 7th centuries, it is not physically impressive for those with little interest in the site's history. The former settlement is marked out on the field with narrow concrete paths, showing where the walls had been. It may have been the site of a pre-Christian temple, from the details found at the burial enclosure. A timber hall had been built, probably for a local Anglo-Saxon lord. There is evidence that the hall was destroyed by fire after fifty to a hundred years' use, but quickly rebuilt.

Greyfriar's Kirk

In the heart of Edinburgh's Old Town, this small church has no steeple, so it's not as easy to find. Look for Greyfriars Bobby's Bar, and you will see the passage to the church. It is a beautiful building, restored with lovely stained-glass windows. The National Covenant was signed here in 1638, but there are other reasons it is so well known.

You can find the grave of policeman John Gray, whose Skye Terrier, Bobby, aka Greyfriar's Bobby, waited there every day for fourteen years, until his own death. There is a small statue of the wee dog in front of the pub, and a Disney movie made about the story.

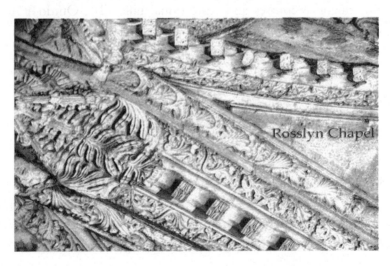

Rosslyn Chapel

Museum of Fire

Many people don't realize that Edinburgh was the location of the first municipal fire brigade in Europe. This museum helps recount that history, between 1824 and the 1940s. There are engines, equipment, and uniforms on display for the visitor. You can see horse-drawn pumps, hand-pulled pumps, and all sorts of interesting and antique equipment. There are also poignant memorials to those lost in fighting fires throughout the years, including one to those firefighters lost in New York on 9/11.

It is located on the ground floor of the Lothian and Borders Fire and Rescue Service. Do not be fooled by the modest exterior, as it hides a much larger interior area.

Underground Edinburgh

There are a couple of attractions, such as The Real Mary King's Close and the Edinburgh Vaults.

- **The Real Mary King's Close.** Who doesn't love a good ghost story? Especially if the location is creepy and quiet even in the bustle of the modern world? In the 1600s, this warren of underground streets was closed off to prevent the spreading of plague. It is filled with mystery, tales of ghosts and cruel horrors. You can tour the area with a costumed guide with a flair for the melodramatic.
- **The Edinburgh Vaults**. This is a series of chambers underneath the city of Edinburgh itself, formed from almost twenty arches of the South Bridge, built in 1788. These vaults used to hold all manner of shops, hold smuggled goods, and hidden bodies. Ghost tours are conducted through here as well, and end at a venue called The Caves and The Rowantree.

It was named after a prominent businesswoman in the 1630s, a widow who traded in fabrics. The ghosts reputed to haunt the area include a young girl, and countless dolls and toys have been left to placate her troubled spirit over the years.

Rosslyn Chapel

Everything you've heard about this place is true, the carvings are amazing and incredible. It's a small place, and yes, the outside is covered with a permanent canopy to protect the stonework from the elements. But the carvings are mostly on the inside and will take your breath away. No surface in this church has been left uncarved. Little angels cavort on the columns, devils carved upside down. Also, around the chapel you'll find hand-carved figures of animals, human figures, and items from nature such as seashells and sheaves of corn and wheat.

You can't help but notice the Apprentice Pillar, the only spiral structural support in the chapel. As the story goes, the master stone mason was going away for a few days and told his apprentices he wanted to be impressed when he returned, create pillars of hand carved stonework to impress him. On his return, one apprentice had created a spiral pillar. So jealous did the master mason become that he took up a hammer and bludgeoned the apprentice to death. The master mason was arrested and put to death. There are three faces around the church, the master mason, the apprentice with a hammer mark on his forehead, and that of the grieving mother.

Edinburgh Castle

A basement crypt is also open which features the tomb of the 2nd Earl of Rosslyn who died in 1837. He wished to be buried in the original vault, variously rumored to be the resting place of Jesus Christ's head, the Holy Grail, and/or the Treasures of the Templars (reputed to be the original Scottish Crown Jewels). An exhaustive search was made, but no entrance to the original vault was found, so he was buried beside his wife in the Lady Chapel, which is entered into through a small door near the altar.

Rosslyn was used in the filming of the movie, *The DaVinci Code*, which has reinvigorated interest in this site.

Royal Botanic Gardens

If you are intimidated by the hustle and bustle of Edinburgh, go for a relaxing walk in the gardens! It started in 1670 as a physic garden for medicinal plants. Now it includes an herbarium, alpine plants, a Chinese Hillside, glasshouses with several different environments on display, rainforest plants, peat walls, waterfalls, a Scottish Heath garden, and many more. Entrance is free, though there is a small charge to go into the glasshouses.

There are four Royal Botanic Gardens around Scotland: in Edinburgh, Dawyck, Logan, and Benmore, and each has a particular collection of plantlife. The total collection numbers more than thirteen thousand living plant species, and the herbarium has over three million preserved specimens.

Scotch Whisky Experience, On the Royal Mile in Edinburgh, stop in to sample some drams! This is no staid, standing around tour, gazing at empty barrels and sealed vats. Take The Silver Tour in a whisky barrel ride through the production plant, being part of the process of making whisky, discovering the history of the drink, and experience the different flavors the regions and locations impart to this amber liquid. Samples are available at the end, though the children are given Irn Bru, which has an indescribable flavor with a medicinal aftertaste similar to ginger. It must be tasted to be appreciated.

St. Margaret's Chapel, Edinburgh Castle

Edinburgh Castle itself is far from a hidden gem. Indeed, the imposing structure juts up out of the hills of the city like a sentry and crowning the medieval heart of Edinburgh. However, St. Margaret's is the oldest part of the site, and is quite tiny and peaceful. It dates to circa 12th century, and likely built for St. Margaret's son, David I. It was restored in the 19th century to the form it is today. Robert the Bruce captured the castle in 1314 and destroyed all of the buildings except for this chapel. On his deathbed in 1329, Bruce issued orders for the chapel's repaint, leaving some forty pounds for restoration. From that time, the chapel was known as "The Royal Chapel of the Castle."

There are several beautiful stained-glass windows, including one of St. Brendan the Navigator, an Irish explorer monk from the 5th century. Other windows show St. Andrew, St. Margaret, St. Columba, St. Ninian, and William Wallace. They were created by the artist Douglas Strachan.

Stone of Destiny

Also known as The Stone of Scone and The Coronation Stone, for centuries it was used in the coronation of Scottish monarchs, and later those of England and Great Britain. The stone was last used in 1953 for the coronation of Elizabeth II. There are many tales and legends about this stone, including that in 1314, who was then the King of Munster, Cormac McCarthy, is said to have sent four thousand soldiers to aid Robert the Bruce at the Battle of Bannockburn. Bruce showed his gratitude by gifting McCarthy with half the Stone of Destiny. While this is a very romantic story and quite believable, the Stone of Destiny is actually red sandstone while the Blarney Stone is bluestone, another type of sandstone, which puts this romantic story to rest.

Regardless of its origins (geologically, from Scone, hence the name Stone of Scone), it was taken by Edward I to Westminster and placed under the throne until 1996, when it was returned to Edinburgh Castle. A replica stone can be found at Scone Palace, in Scone near Perth.

Moray

Ardclach Bell Tower

This architectural oddity is quite small, and easily missed. It's only two levels (ground and first floor) and could be mistaken for a prison. And in a way it probably was. This structure dates to 1655, according to a stone slab on the gable end opposite the bell tower, and was built by Alexander Brodie of Lethen, a Covenanter, a small 17th century Presbyterian movement. Brodie's religious beliefs made him a traitor to King Charles I, and as a result his lands and property were repeatedly sacked in 1645. He built this tower as a means of defense. The tower stands on a hill with a lovely, albeit strategic, view. On an interior wall are the stone carved initials, MGB, Margaret Grant Brodie, who was Alexander's second wife. The summit of the hill is so small that it was terraced on one side to bolster the footprint of the tower. The tower was eventually acquired by the Ardclach church to use as a bell tower, which was added at that time, presumably because the high elevation meant the sound of the bell would be heard in a much greater distance than from the church in the valley. However, that never happened, and in 1838 when the building was restored, it continued as a belfry but was never used for the purpose in which it was meant.

Auchindoun Castle

This 15th century ruined tower castle was built on the remains of an Iron Age hillfort; there are prehistoric and Pictish earthworks on these grounds. It was built by Thomas Cochran, who later became the Earl of Mar. It was then passed to the Clan Ogilvy in 1489, and then onto Clan Gordon in 1535. Following the Restoration of Charles II, the castle was again awarded to the Marquis of Huntly. It was destroyed by the Clan MacKintosh in 1592. Many of the stones were removed and used elsewhere in the region, including Balvenie Castle. It was totally derelict by 1725 and has never been restored, though the remaining ruins are still impressive.

At one point, the site contained a stable, brewery, bakery, and cellars, and the dungeons, which were carved into the bedrock beneath the tower. Condemned for many years as too dangerous, the structure was stabilized and opened to the public in 2007.

Brodie Castle

This restored manor house, home to the Brodie family, was originally built in 1567, but destroyed in a fire less than one hundred years later. It was rebuilt and expanded in the early 19th century when the manor house was added onto the castle and is now very well preserved and open to visitors, weddings and events. The interior is truly impressive, with all sorts of magnificent details, such as the Victorian kitchen, the day nursery, complete with a children's cooking range, and a dining room. In true Victorian fashion, the attention to detail, particularly on the dining room ceiling, is incredible.

There is an ancient Pictish monument on the grounds called Rodney's Stone, a two-yard-high cross slab with carvings on both sides. One side has a cross, and the other, symbols of fish monsters, a beast, and a double disc. The stone has an inscription, the longest of all Pictish inscriptions, in Ogham writing. While some of it is weathered beyond legibility, some does contain the name of a Pictish Saint, St. Ethernan.

Burghead Promontory Fort and Well

Unfortunately, most of this impressive structure was dismantled and built over in the early 19th century, to create homes for those displaced in the Highland Clearances. However, what remains is still impressive. The fort was likely the seat of power for the Pictish Kingdom of Fortriu and was in its glory from circa 300 to 800 CE. The fortress was originally seven-and-a-half acres large, and contained a chambered well, probably used in ritual. Many carved Pictish stones were part of the original structure, but only a few survived the dismantling. Many had bull carvings, a symbol not normally found in other Pictish carvings, they became known as the Burghead Bulls. Those few are now housed in the visitor center, which also recreates the former glory of the site.

Elgin Cathedral

Majestic and imposing, this spectacular cathedral is stunning even in its ruins. What remains are the bones of its former glory. This cathedral was established in 1224 and dedicated to the Holy Trinity on land granted by King Alexander II, replacing the cathedral at Spynie a few miles away. It was staffed by eighteen canons by 1226 which increased to twenty-three by 1242.

Through the centuries, the church suffered through sackings and burnings, but increased its size with each restoration. And by 1560, the time of the Scottish Reformation, the number of canons had increased to twenty-five. Elgin Catheral became the second largest cathedral in Scotland, behind St Andrews which was the largest. As a result of the Reformation, the cathedral was abandoned, and its services transferred to the parish church of St. Giles. Once the lead waterproofing was removed from the room in 1567, the church quickly fell into ruin and rapid decay.

The site was tidied in Victorian times, a time when visiting graveyards came into fashion, but the church was never restored, and remains open today for casual visitors. Notable mentions are the intact Chapter House and its elegant, vaulted ceiling, the Pictish Cross Slab, and the stone figures of a bishop and a knight in the nave. While you can climb to the top of the north tower, beware if you suffer vertigo.

Nairnshire

Cawdor Castle

This restored late 4th century castle dates back to circa 1180 when the first Thane of Cawdor, or Calder as it was originally spelled, was appointed Sheriff and Hereditary Constable of the royal castle at Nairn. Thane is the equivalent of baron. The keep received its license to fortify in 1454. It's unknown who originally built the first structure, but by this time it was well in the possession of Calders, and William Calder, the 6th Thane of Cawdor. This site has some unique features, including being built around a small living holly tree. Legend says that a donkey laden with gold laid down to rest under the tree, and the site for the castle was chosen. The remains of that tree are still evident in the lowest chamber in the castle, called the Thorn Tree Room.

The castle is associated with Shakespeare's Macbeth, as he was hailed as the Thane of Cawdor by the three witches. However, the true Macbeth died one hundred and thirty years before the title existed and was likely changed subsequently from the Thane of Cromarty.

There is a gift shop onsite, as well as a book shop, a wool shop, and restaurant. The extensive estate and walled garden are open to visitors, as well as the golf course and natural woodlands.

Clava Cairns

Clava Cairns

Nearby Culloden, you can find the Clava Cairns. The Clava cairn is a type of Bronze Age circular chamber tomb cairn and named after the group of three cairns at Balnuaran of Clava. There were several cairns and stone circles in Clava, and it was a fascinating place, even in the bright sunlight. The stones themselves had many interesting patterns on them, not necessarily carved patterns, but the stones themselves and the lichen growing on them were lovely. One is covered in cup marks, small manmade concave indentations.

Nairn Beach

Low sand dunes and a promenade stretch along the Nairn coastline, making this a lovely walking beach, where you can look across the Moray Firth to the Black Isles. If you fancy a long walk, there is a nearby nature reserve with several coastal walks. It is a great family picnic spot. There is a resident school of dolphins in the water itself.

Orkney

While this may seem like a long way to travel, the Orkneys have many lovely places to visit, explore, and experience. There are countless

Neolithic and Viking sites to see, as well as a wonderful mix of Pictish and Norse culture throughout the islands.

Balfour Castle

Located in the Orkney Islands on Shapinsay, this is the most northerly castle hotel in the world. It's a Victorian structure, built on an island you can reach by ferry from Kirkwall. The village was created to support the estate in the late 18th century and offers lovely views of the other islands from Ward Hill.

The castle itself has turrets, a castellated tower, and large picture windows.

There are several historic outbuildings, such as a smithy, gatehouse, gashouse, and the largest water-powered grinding mill in Orkney. There is a standing stone called *Mòr Stein*, standing at three yards high, said to have been thrown from the mainland by a giant, after his fleeing wife. There is a chambered Cairn with the colorful name of Castle Bloody. The Broch of Burroughston is a Pictish tower.

Bishop's & Earl's Palaces

Located in the town of Kirkwall, these palaces are considered two of the best examples of architecture in Scotland and show both Norse and ecclesiastical elements. The fireplace, in particular, is spectacular. The front façade has a complex array of corbeled turrets and oriel windows.

The Bishop's Palace was built by the Stewarts, at the same time as St. Magnus' Cathedral (see below), and is where King Haakon IV died, marking the end of Norse rule in the Outer Hebrides. The Earl's Palace was built in the early 1600s, mostly by forced labor, when the Lord of Orkney felt the Bishop's Palace no longer suited his needs.

Complicating matters, the Stewarts did not actually own the land on which they built! While under arrest, his son waged a battle to claim the land and capture the palace, but he too was arrested, and both father and son were eventually executed. The properties eventually fell into the hands of the Crown and went to ruin by the 18th century. Though the roof is missing, it retains some of the elegance of its original Renaissance architecture.

Blackhammer Cairn

This chambered cairn on Rousay in Orkney has gotten a reconstructed concrete roof to protect the remains of the cairn from the elements. Seven chambers are divided by upright stone slabs, set in a distinctive decorative design. This triangular design is mirrored in Unstan pottery patterns from the area. The roof has translucent panels to let light into the chambers, but you can still see the cairn walls and chambers with the original construction. Some of the items discovered in the cairn are flint knives, remains of an Unstan urn, animal bones and the remains of two humans.

Broch of Gurness/Midhowe Broch

This is a Pictish tower with a very large and complex footprint, on the edge of a windswept and stormy coast. It was inhabited until circa 100 CE, and likely housed an extended family. It was probably used as a last defensive resort for an entire surrounding village, though, during times of attack. There is evidence that it was used as a Viking burial site in later years, from grave goods and human remains. You might also want to check out the nearby Midhowe Broch across the Eynhallow Sound on Rousay. This one stands on a tall cliff and is well excavated with extensive outbuildings.

You can catch exceptional views here. You can sometimes spy seals in the waters below the cliff, perhaps on the small sandy beach.

Brough of Birsay

Occupied by first the Picts and then the Norse, this important center is only accessible at low tide. The parking lot is at the Point of Buckquoy, and then steps take you to the natural causeway. *Make sure you have time to return before the tide does!*

An enclosure around the Norse church surrounds the Pictish graveyard, and there is a symbol stone left from their legacy. The stone portrays Pictish nobles in long robes, bearing weapons and shields. There are church remains, dedicated to St. Peter, from about eleven hundred years ago. There may have been a monastery on the grounds at one point, as well as a possible sauna and bathhouse.

Don't miss visiting the small Romanesque church, which dates back to the 12th century. Dedicated to St. Peter, it is made of fine red sandstone. It was a pilgrimage site and may have replaced an earlier Pictish holy place. While it is square at one end, the other end is a semi-circular apse.

Brough of Deerness

No one is certain what the Brough of Deerness was, originally. It could have been a pre-Norse Christian settlement, or it could be an Iron Age cliff top fortification. In the 1970s, excavators uncovered the remains of a chapel dating back to the pre-Norse period, which now stand about four or five feet high.

Extensive excavations in 2008 revealed the site was a Viking chieftain's settlement. It was definitely domestic, as the artifacts found were spindles, pottery, loom weights, etc. However, there is still a possibility that it covered an earlier structure.

The peninsula this Brough is on just clings to the eastern edge of the main Orkney Island, only attached by a strip of sand bar. On the way to the Brough, you can see The Gloup, what used to be a sea cave, but is now collapsed into a deep gorge. A bit of scrambling is required, but it is reasonably accessible to the able-bodied. Covenanters' Memorial is a memorial to the two hundred Covenanters who drowned along the coast when their prison ship foundered in a storm.

Hoy

Churchill Barriers

During WWII, operations for the Navy fleet were moved to Scapa Flow, in the Orkneys. In order to guard the approach to the base, a series of four causeways were built here, with a total length of one-and-a-half miles. They link the northern part of Orkney mainland to the island of South Ronaldsay via Burray and the two smaller islands of Lamb Holm and Glimps Holm.

These barriers were built primarily as naval defenses to protect the anchorage at Scapa Flow, but they now serve as road links, carrying the A961 road from Kirkwall to Burwick. There is a series of sunken ships and debris between the islands, deliberately sunk by Churchill to keep enemy submarines from getting to the fleet. These rusting wrecks are still visible even at high tide, with bits sticking up through the water.

Italian Chapel

The Italian Chapel was built by Italian POWs out of a Quonset hut and scraps of iron. They painted the inside as if it was lined in tiles, in true Trompe l'Oeil style, and created ironwork for the inside, making a magical religious wonderland inside. Sadly, it was only used as a chapel for a couple years, but I am very glad the folks of Orkney were smart and kind enough to have preserved this little gem.

Maes Howe

Maeshowe

This Neolithic structure may have originally been a standing stone site, as the four corners of the interior have standing stones with carvings. It is considered the finest chambered tomb in the northwest of Europe, and predates the Egyptian pyramids.

There is a guided tour here which I highly recommend. The guide offers a great deal of history about the area, the tomb, its discovery, and the various people who had occupied it. Viking writing on the walls that differed little from modern day graffiti, including suggestive innuendos, is translated through the guide. One translation suggested, "Ivar has a huge axe."

The tunnel is low and long, so a bit of stooping is required. There is enough room for perhaps twenty people to stand inside (a bit snugly), but it is well worth some time. It is a fascinating glimpse into two distinct cultures, the original Neolithic builders, and the Vikings, four thousand years later. At sunset on winter solstice, the entire length of the passage lights up with the sun shining on the rear wall of the central chamber.

Old Man of Hoy

UK's tallest sea stack, the Old Man rises out of the sea at four hundred and fifty feet and can usually be seen from the ferry to Orkney, if the conditions are clear enough. The striations in the red sandstone give it a dramatic appearance, especially in the rain, as the colors are vibrant and stunning.

The Old Man is probably less than two hundred and fifty years old. It is not mentioned in the Orkneyinga Saga, written circa 1230. On the Blaeu map of 1600 CE, a headland exists to the point where the Old Man is now. The McKenzie map of Hoy of 1750 similarly shows a headland but no stack, though by 1819, the Old Man had been separated from the mainland.

Artist William Daniell sketched the sea stack at this time as a wider column with a smaller top section and an arch at the base, giving the form legs. A short time later, a storm washed away one of the legs leaving it much as it is today, although erosion continues. In 1992 a one-hundred-and-thirty-foot crack appeared in the top of the south face, leaving a large overhanging section that will eventually collapse. This has not deterred climbers and base jumpers, and film crews.

Orphir Church & The Earl's Bú

Off a side road near the Hoy ferry terminus, this odd little round church ruin is near the Orkneyinga Saga Centre, celebrating the Viking heritage of the area. It is the only surviving circular medieval church in Scotland. The church was modeled after the rotunda of the Church of the Holy Sepulchre in Jerusalem. Most of the church was destroyed to build the nearby church in 1757, and that is also now long gone.

In the Orkneyinga Saga, written in 1136 CE, there is an account of a great Yule feast given by Earl Paul at his bú, or residence, at Orphirs: *"There was a large drinking-hall; the door was near the east gable on the southern wall, and a magnificent church stood before the hall door, and one had to go down to the church from the hall."* The remains of that "magnificent church" are dedicated to St Nicholas and still survive.

The Bú was a manor house in the 1100s of the Norse Earls of Orkney, and the Round Church of St. Nicholas is just near it. There isn't much left of either, but there are some walls and foundations marked. There is a great collection of gravestones and markers, as well as lovely views over the Scapa Flow.

Ring of Brodgar

Ring of Brodgar

Any trip to Orkney would be incomplete without a visit to this site. It's not a hidden site, but it is worth a mention because it is truly impressive. The large circle of stones, measuring one hundred and fourteen yards in diameter, lies just north of the Stenness Stones on the main Orkney Island. There is an earthen ditch around the stones, and the very flat surrounding land and islands make it seem like you can skip stones for miles, just hitting each small island on the way.

The site has never been fully excavated or scientifically dated, so it remains shrouded in mystery and myth. However, it is likely that it was built between 2500 and 2000 BCE. It is thought it originally had sixty stones, but only twenty-seven remain. It's the third largest circle in the British Isles, after Avebury and Stanton Drew.

Recent ongoing excavations in the nearby Ness of Brodgar have revealed an extensive domestic complex of Neolithic buildings, artwork, pottery, bones and tools, in an area of about six acres. The site dates from circa 3,200 to 2,300 BCE, which makes it concurrent with the building of the Ring of Brodgar.

St. Magnus Cathedral

The word of the day is RED! Red and white sandstone make this 12th century cathedral, the carvings of which would be spectacular anyway, unique and exquisite, especially in the rain when the stone is wet. It is also the most northerly cathedral in the British Isles. There is fantastic curvilinear ironwork on the massive oak doors and soaring Romanesque archways in red sandstone to greet the visitor.

St. Magnus was reputed to be pious and gentle. He refused to fight or raid and was granted a share of the Earldom of Orkney held by his cousin, Haakon. They ruled peaceably for some years until their followers started arguing. An assembly was set to settle the matter, and Haakon brought more ships than they had agreed upon. Magnus was captured and then killed by his treacherous cousin.

The interior has more curvilinear designs, this time carved from stone, throughout the chapel. This is the largest building in Kirkwall, smack in the center of town, and a fantastic rallying point for groups that wander, or a base for giving directions through the winding streets of the city. It should be noted that St. Magnus is not owned by the church, but by the burgh of Kirkwall. This was a result of an act of King James III of Scotland following Orkney's annexation in 1468 by the Scottish Crown. And it has its own dungeon!

Scapa Flow

This body of water is sheltered by a string of islands around the main Orkney Island. It has a shallow sandy bottom and is therefore a great natural harbor. Viking ships used it a thousand years ago, and it was pivotal in the Wars of the Three Kingdoms in 1650. In WWI and WWII, it was Britain's chief naval base, until it closed in 1956. Its protected location was considered ideal against German submarine threats, once Churchill sunk ships in nearby channels to form the Churchill Barriers.

Skara Brae

Skara Brae

Known as the Scottish Pompeii, this site is truly impressive, and a must-see for anyone in this corner of Scotland.

Most of the sites we see from this time period are religious in nature, like Stonehenge or the Pyramids. But this site feels very homey, with chambers and hearths. Catch a glimpse into what everyday life may have been like for people who lived here, and realize it wasn't all that different from ours today.

There is also a small café, a visitor center, and a mock-up of the site.

Included in the ticket for Skara Brae is Skaill House, a grand mansion that has stood since the 1600s, and has an eclectic collection of artifacts, from Captain Cook's dinner service to a Viking calendar stick.

Stenness Stones

Dated to circa 3,100 BCE, this is one of the oldest stone circles in Britain. The tallest stone stands at nineteen feet, truly dwarfing all around it. Located near the center of the main Orkney Island, this set of standing stones is on a farm on a tiny neck of land leading to the Ring of Brodgar. It is very easy to explore, as there's a parking lot right next to it. The views of the surrounding islands and inlets are magnificent, and if you are lucky enough to get there on a summer solstice, you will have to be there very late to see the sun set (after midnight!).

Tradition states that, during the five days of feasting around New Year, lovers can visit the Stenness Stones. The woman kneels and prays to the "God Wodden" that she and her partner will keep the oaths they are about to swear. Then they go to the Ring of Brodgar and repeat the ritual pact before the Odin Stone.

Stenness Stones

Tomb of the Eagles

Also known as Isbister Chambered Cairn, got its nickname from the number of sea eagle bones found within the tomb when it was excavated. It's a long drive to the end of the island string from the main Orkney Island, but it's worth the drive, and the mile hike. Not just for the tomb, but for the incredible angular cliffs and seabirds which inhabit the area. Everything is at an angle, which is how the tomb was discovered, the tomb stones were straight and seemed out of place. To get into the tomb, you have to lay on a wheeled board and pull yourself into the tomb on a rope, but once inside, it's high enough to stand in. Interior lighting is provided through skylights. The walk back along the cliffs is highly recommended. There are plenty of seabirds, and wildflowers dot the landscape from spring through summer.

Unstan Cairn

This cairn is on a promontory near the Stenness Loch, near the Ring of Brodgar. This one is similar on the outside to Maeshowe, but inside the architecture is different. There are large flagstone slabs dividing the main chamber into circular stalls, giving them the classification of "stalled tombs." The roof is a modern concrete construction with a skylight, offering natural interior light. In construction, it's a hybrid of the Maeshowe chambered tomb and the Orkney-Cromarty design of circular tombs.

The name Unstan was given to the large amount of pottery scattered around the floor. There were at least thirty Neolithic bowls in the tomb, distinctive by their round bottoms and linear decorations. They were found along with human and animal bones.

Vat of Kirbister

On the island of Stronsay in Orkney, this rock arch is the roof of a very large, almost circular cave that's collapsed. There is a lay-by nearby to park in, and then a path runs between fields to get to this inlet.

While visiting the arch, don't miss the nearby sea stack called the Malme which houses the remains of an early Christian hermitage. While you can get quite close to the arch, a fence is placed to keep visitors off the precarious rocks. There is another sea stack nearby, called Tam's Castle, with another hermitage on top. These early Christians evidently went to a great deal of trouble to guarantee their solitude.

Peeblesshire

Dawyck House and Botanical Garden

This 13th century manor house was built by the Veitch Family, and then passed on to the Balfours. It was destroyed in 1830 but rebuilt. It has extensive botanical gardens as well as a chapel to explore. The gardens are about sixty acres along the River Tweed and have one of the best arboretums in the world, due to three hundred years of tree collecting by three different families. Walk along the Beech Walk or explore the Azalea Terrace.

They are part of the three gardens that form the Royal Botanic Gardens, along with Edinburgh, Benmore Botanic Gardens, and Logan Botanic Gardens.

Loch Tay

Stobo Kirk

Dedicated to St. Mungo, and probably founded in the 6th century, it is one of the oldest standing churches in Scotland. While it is a Protestant church, it retains many of the splendid décor of the Catholic churches, including the door made from cedar of Lebanon, 17th century brass hanging lamps, and the beautiful stained-glass windows. Don't miss churchyard gravestones and carvings, some of which are unusual and fascinating, such as Robert Vesey's grave marker, or that of John Noble and his musket.

The legend says that St. Mungo, also known as St. Kentigern, converted *Myrddin Wilt* (Merlin) to Christianity and baptized him on a boulder. That boulder was made into the altar stone at Stobo.

Robert Smail's Printing Works

This is a fully functional Victorian letterpress printer, showing the operations of a 19th century printer. Smails ran a weekly newspaper between 1893 and 1916 and was opened to the public in 1990. There is a tour showing the stages of the printing process, as well as some hands-on workshops. Exhibits of stationery, writing slates, sealing wax, letter cases and compositors tell you all you want to know about the printing trade of the time.

Perthshire

Beatrix Potter Exhibition

Escape back to the days of your childhood or introduce your own children to the world of Peter Rabbit. This extensive exhibition in Dunkeld is a great stop for the young, or just young at heart. This is a place where your favorite characters come alive, and the world of Beatrix Potter comes to life. If the weather is poor, enjoy the indoor exhibition, along with the tearoom and gift shop for a break.

Black Watch Museum

Located within Balhousie Castle in Perth, this museum is open all year, and tells the story of Scotland's best known military regiment, which goes back three hundred years. There are gardens, a gift shop and a café to relax in, as well as a collection of paintings, artifacts and photographs to explain the history.

Blair Castle & Gardens

Blair Castle had a rather intriguing start. In 1269, while David I Strathbogie, Earl of Atholl, was called away to the Crusades, his northern neighbor, John I Comyn, Lord of Badenoch, began building on the Earl's land. When the Earl returned and found what his neighbor was doing, he complained to King Alexander III and won back his lands.

He then incorporated the new tower into an extension to his own home. David II Strathbogie, Earl of Atholl, was eventually forced to forfeit his titles and estates after rebelling against Robert the Bruce in 1322. The earldom was granted to a number of individuals until 1457 when James II granted it to his half-brother, John Stewart. In 1629, John Murray, son of the second Earl of Tullibardine, was created Earl of Atholl, and the title has remained in the Murray family ever since. This spectacular white turreted castle is considered the ancestral home of Clan Murray. The current Duke of Atholl, John Murray, lives in South Africa, and his father had given the estate into a charitable trust to be left under Scottish control. It is open to the public, and the restored rooms have collections of weapons, trophies, paintings, furniture, and tapestries. It is the garrison for the Atholl Highlanders, the Duke's private army, and the only legal private army in Europe.

Dunfallandy Stone

A Pictish cross slab that stands alone about a mile south of Pitlochry, this ancient carving is accessible from a small road just off the A9. The walk is a couple of hundred yards past a farmhouse and a bit of a climb.

The stone itself is under a glass and stone structure for protection from the elements. It stands about five feet high, and dates to about the 700s. There is an elaborate cross carved on the face, with symbols and figures on the other side, with angels and animals. Fish-tailed snakes form a frame around the images of symbols and figures. The figures on one side are thought by some to be St. Paul and St. Anthony. It is known locally as *Clach an t'Sagairt*, or The Priest's Stone.

Dunkeld Cathedral

The current church was established in 1260 but not completed until 1501. Located on the north bank of the River Tay, this location has been holy ground since at least 730 CE, when Culdees (Celtic missionaries) built a monastery here. The King of Scots and Picts, Kenneth MacAlpin, had the original church rebuilt in 848 CE.

Dunkeld became the religious center of Scotland when the relics of St. Columba were moved here, after Viking attacks ravaged the monasteries of the west coast. The current cathedral has both Gothic and Norman architecture, reflecting its various histories in a fascinating contrast due to the length of time it took to complete. It holds several ancient carvings, such as the Apostle's Stone, the Old Bell and the Pictish Cross Slab, from circa 800 CE.

Falls of Dochart

While this is a fast-flowing river, there are areas slow enough to allow climbing onto some of the rocks. On either side, there are interesting buildings, the Breadalbane Folklore Centre and the Falls of Dochart Inn. While the folklore center started as a mill, the inn started out as a blacksmithy in the late 19th century.

The Bridge of Dochart, built in 1760, crosses the river to Killin. From the bridge, you will see the cascades of falls, and an island called Innis Bhuidhe, which is the burial place of the Clan McNab. In the center of the grounds, you will find an oblong enclosure which holds the burials of nine of the clan chiefs.

Finlarig Castle

With a rather bloody history, the ruins of this castle are hidden away along a deep forest path along the River Lochay, near Killin. It was built in 1629 by "Black" Duncan Campbell, of the Campbells of Breadalbane. It includes a stone-lined pit, legendarily used for beheading prisoners of noble blood. Commoners were not accorded such courtesy, though; they were hanged on a nearby oak tree. Finlarig's most notorious visitor was Rob Roy who reputedly stayed here in 1713.

Nearby are the remnants of the Breadalbane Mausoleum, built circa 1830 in a mock-Tudor style. This mausoleum was built over a former church and burial grounds which had been established in 1523.

Explore both areas with caution, as these are not maintained ruins, and loose stones are likely.

The Hermitage Pleasure Ground

Located near Dunkeld, this lovely forest is home to Ossian's Hall of Mirrors, Ossian's Cave, and others are Georgian follies built by the Dukes of Atholl. Ossian was a blind bard in Celtic legend, styled after the Irish bard, Oisín. The Hermit's Cave was built circa 1760 for the Earl of Breadalbane to honor the bard. He advertised, unsuccessfully, for a permanent hermit to live there, basically as a tourist attraction.

The riverside walk is about a mile to Ossian's Hall, which overlooks a triple waterfall. There is also a thirty-mile network of paths beyond that, which date to the 18th century. A stone foot bridge from 1770 is near the Black Linn Falls.

Two interesting features are found here, a Douglas Fir tree which, was recorded as the tallest tree in Britain at two hundred feet, and beside the 1770s bridge is a Cedar of Lebanon, which is meant to be the oldest living tree in the hermitage, dating back to around the time of the bridge's construction.

Inchmahome Priory

Huntingtower Castle

Once known as Ruthven Castle and the Palace of Ruthven, it was built in the 15th century by the Clan Ruthven, Earls of Gowrie. The Earl of Gowrie was involved in a plot to kidnap the son of Mary Queen of Scots, the young King James VI. The successful ten-month kidnapping was known as the Raid of Ruthven. In later years, Gowrie was implicated again in a plan to kill the king, and was summarily executed, his properties and titles all confiscated.

The castle is made up of two towers, the Eastern Tower (once the servants' quarters) and the Western Tower (once the family quarters). Of some of the surviving features in the castle, the greatest of them can be found in the Eastern Tower. These include early 16th century wall painting on the tower's first floor; fragments showing flora and fauna, and Biblical scenes. As well, there are decorative paintings on the timber ceiling which include Renaissance-style knotwork patterns on overlaying planks, and grotesques (animal versions of the traditional Green Man). The ceiling is thought to be the earliest surviving example of this style of art in Scotland. There are less impressive wall-paintings in the Western Tower but definitely worth seeing.

Inchmahome Priory

The castle has an interesting history with the Murray and Ruthven families, and a romantic story associated with the gap between the two towers, known as The Maiden's Leap, which gets its name from a daring leap made by the Earl's daughter, Dorthea. As the legend goes, Dorthea was in love with one of the servants and used a bridge between the towers to visit him. One night, her mother, the Countess, followed Dorthea who escaped to the roof, as there was no other passage back to her chamber. From the roof, she leapt from the battlement onto a landing on the Western Tower and rushed to her chamber, where her mother found her. The following day, Dorthea and her lover eloped. There are no records of what happened to Dorthea after that night. However, visitors have said they've seen the ghost of a young woman in a green silk dress walking the halls. Her sighting is usually an omen that death is to come to those who see her.

Some castles are famous for ghosts, however, Huntingtower is also famous for its bats. There is a colony of pipistrelle bats, which are the smallest bat in Europe. Visitors are warned the bats are not house-trained, evident by their leavings, so children should be watched during a visit.

The castle has been carefully restored but is not furnished. You will see the bare stone walls (once plastered), hearths, and windows without the trappings of everyday life.

Inchmahome Priory

Located on an island in the Lake of Menteith, this serene, ruined abbey is well worth the short boat ride from the mainland. Technically, this is the only Lake in Scotland, as it was named by an Englishman; all the rest are lochs.

The Priory was founded in 1238 by the powerful Comyn family as an Augustinian Order and has had an interesting list of visitors over the centuries. Some of the most notable include King Robert the Bruce who stayed here on three occasions, 1306, 1308, 1310, possibly for political purposes, as the Priory at the time had sworn allegiance to King Edward I of England.

The priory also served as refuge in 1547 for Queen Mary, who was four years of age at the time. The young Mary was hidden here following the disastrous defeat of the Scots army at the Battle of Pinkie Cleugh during the Rough Wooing. The Rough Wooing was a conflict which arose when Henry VIII declared war against the Scots in an effort to force a marriage between his son, Edward, and the infant, Mary, who would later become known as Mary, Queen of Scots. In Scotland, this war was called the Eight Years War, and also the Nine Years War. The term "rough wooing" is attributed to George Gordon, 4th Earl of Huntly, who is quoted as saying, "We liked not the manner of the wooing, and we could not stoop to being bullied into love." Later, the term "wooing" was popularized by Sir Walter Scott, and the phrase "rough wooing" was commonly seen in books from the mid-19th century.

The Priory fell into ruin after the Reformation, but this is a wonderful site to explore. The Chapter House is the best-preserved structure on the site, largely as it had been converted into a family mausoleum in the 18th century by the Graham family. You will see several fine carved medieval effigies which were placed here for preservation.

Make sure to explore the vaulted ground floor of the kitchen. There is a small forest on the island that is worthy of exploration and serene reflection. If you are there in the right time of year, the forest floor is covered in bluebells.

Keillor Symbol Stone

The stone is six feet five inches in height, and only carved on the side facing the road. It is well situated in a flat area, and visible for miles. The carvings include a double disc and Z-rod, which may represent the dynasty of a line of Pictish kings, sort of like a coat of arms.

The burial of a woman's bones and carvings of a less distinct mirror and comb symbol indicate it might be the burial tomb of a noblewoman, but that is open to speculation. At the top is the carving of an animal, either a wolf or a bear, with his mouth open. The stone is estimated at twelve hundred years of age.

Meikleour Beech Hedge

If you have an urge to feel small and insignificant, seek out this odd hedge. Since 1966, this has been recognized as the tallest and longest hedge on Earth. These beech trees average one hundred feet in height and stretch along the roadside for one-third of a mile. The hedge was planted in 1745 by Robert Murray Nairne and his wife, Jean Mercer of Meikleour, shortly before the arrival of Bonnie Prince Charlie to Scotland. It is said that the beech trees stand tall and straight towards heaven because the men who helped plant the hedge were killed at the Battle of Culloden. It takes four men six weeks and a hydraulic lift to trim the hedge.

Tynreich Stone Circle

The word "Tynreich" comes from the old Gaelic name *Tigh nà Ruaich*, or "The House of the Heather." This place is hidden in plain sight, near Ballinluig in Perthshire. It's not that easy to find, but is actually on the grounds of Tynreich Nursery, so check opening times before visiting. This compact stone circle has six stones and is just shy of twenty-two feet in diameter. The largest stone is triangular with ice cracking on the face of it. The excavation in 1855 revealed four ceramic urns with cremated remains, but those have been lost over time.

Blackhouse Interior

Renfrewshire

Castle Semple Loch

This loch is approximately one-and-a-half miles in length, at the eastern end of which are the ruins of Castle Semple, built sometime between 1490 and 1520. There are many attractions around the loch, including a watersports center, a bird sanctuary, and of course, the ruins of the castle which are only accessible by boat. The ruins of a Collegiate Church built in 1505 are situated on the north shore, It still retains the old walled garden. There is the octagonal temple on top of Kenmuir Hill near the house, built as a hunting outlook in the 18th century. Peel Tower on the south shore can also only be reached by boat. This medieval stronghold was likely used by locals as defense against bandits.

Gleniffer Braes

This range of hills south of Paisley is associated with the 18th and 19th century weaver poets of Paisley, such as Robert Tannahill and Hugh MacDonald. The Gleniffer Gorge is situated along the Tannahill Walkway, about fifty feet deep, formed by the Gleniffer Burn. The Craigielinn waterfall is lovely year-round, surrounded by forest and icing up with dramatic stalactites in the winter.

Many birds can be seen in the area, including skylarks, sparrowhawks, goldcrests, and kestrels. Deer and tawny owls are around as well. The Lapwing Lodge Outdoor Centre, circa 1910, was originally set up for Coats Mill workers as a sanatorium. Cycling and horseback riding is encouraged, as well as seasonal activities like Easter egg rolling and sledging.

Arnol Blackhouses

Paisley Abbey

If you love beautiful stained glass and architecture, you should visit Paisley Abbey. Dedicated to Saint Mirren, this community was founded in the 7th century as a Cluniac monastery, a branch of the Benedictines. There are fantastic windows, both ancient and modern, throughout this restored building. While the origins date back to 1163, this building has constantly been updated, and has many lovely sights. The timber ceiling was replaced in 1981 to replace a "temporary" plaster one from 1788.

It's possible the name Paisley comes from the Brythonic word *Passeleg*, meaning "basilica." It is believed that William Wallace may have been educated at the abbey. King Robert II was born there, and possibly through an early caesarean delivery given without anesthesia.

Don't miss the twelve angel corbels and stone communion table or the ceiling bosses. Outside are twelve gargoyles, recently replaced along the southwest cloister, including one modeled after the 1979 film *Alien*.

Ross and Cromarty: The Isles

Arnol Blackhouse Museum and Gearrannan Blackhouse Village

This outdoor museum in the small village of Arnol on the Isle of Lewis consists of several blackhouses, traditional crofter cottages, owes its underlying origins to pre- Roman times. Each cottage shows the

occupation once widespread in the area. Traditionally, this type of cottage had no chimney, so the smoke from the peat fire found its own way out through the thatch. Often livestock would winter inside the cottages, the family on one end and the animals in a byre on the other end. They provided pungent warmth, and waste funneled through a small drainage ditch through the floor. They are called blackhouses to contrast them to the later constructed white houses, newer cottages, which were built during the housing projects of the 1800s.

At the nearby Gearrannan Blackhouse Village you can now rent a blackhouse as a self-catering cottage.

Bostadh Iron Age House

On the island of Great Bernera in the Outer Hebrides, this house was revealed after a storm in 1993 and then excavated. They found the remains of a Norse settlement, and under that, five Pictish houses from about 500 CE. The houses have been nicknamed Jelly Baby or Figure Eight houses, due to their shapes. The construction is fascinating, with double layers of dry stone, with gaps filled with sand, clay, turf, midden, and whatever was on hand.

The original houses have been buried over again to protect them, but a reconstructed house has been erected for visitors. The island is accessible via a road bridge from Lewis. It is located on a sheltered beach inlet.

Calanais

Calanais Stone Circle

Or Callanish, dating back to 2,900-2,600 BCE, the Calanais Stone Circle is probably the most famous stone circle in Scotland. There is a series of several stone circles around the Isle of Lewis, but Calanais I is the largest and most impressive. It's suggested that there were other structures on this site as early as 3000 BCE, but evidence shows the site was abandoned between 2000-1700 BCE.

The circle is made up of thirteen upright stones with a fourteenth stone in center which marks the entrance to a cairn. Stone rows jutting out from the north, south, east, and west form the shape of an uneven Celtic cross. This circle is larger and older than Stonehenge, with an informative visitor center to explain its history.

Calanais II, III, IV, and V are smaller circles nearby, but within sight of Calanais I. Calanais IV and V were down to just a few standing stones, and much more difficult to get to.

Dun Carloway

This is an impressive Iron Age tower with double walls. This is one of the most well-preserved brochs in Scotland, with the highest point in the ruin is nearly thirty feet high. The Morrison clan of Ness suggests this site was in use until around 1601 when current occupants of the fort stole cattle from the MacAuleys of Uig. In retaliation, as the legend goes, Donal Cam MacAuleys used two knives to pull himself up the outer wall, then pushed heather into the broch, setting it alight. This smoked out the inhabitants, and the broch was summarily destroyed.

The site is easily accessible, with a little climb but nothing punishing, and has incredible views of the surrounding area. Its location is fantastic, the land undulated like a disturbed pool. When the sun deems to come out, yellows, golds, oranges, purples, and every other color under the rainbow will appear to jump out at you from the peat bogs and fields.

Dun Carloway

Port Nìs (Ness)

On the northern part of Lewis, the landscape becomes peat bog, a moonscape of undulating brown and gold turf, gently rolling along the top of the land. There are occasional villages along the only road into Ness Village, with white and sandy-stucco houses dotted here and there like lonely outposts to a forgotten civilization. There is a harbor with a fantastic view of the northern Atlantic Ocean, and a lighthouse on a one-hundred-and-seventy-foot cliff with more stunning views.

In the nearby town of Eoropaidh, a restored 6th century church dedicated to St. Moluag. North of the town, a small road takes you to the Butt of Lewis Lighthouse, designed and built by David Stevenson in 1862. Its open brick façade makes a striking contrast to the cliffside.

Shawbost Norse Mill

Also known as the Mill of the Blacksmiths. For a fascinating look at a traditional Norse mill, explore the small thatched, rounded buildings in this traditional museum. It operated for several centuries until 1930, though the last of them was still operational until 1945. Restoration work began in the 1960s, and then again in 1995. Paths were added shortly thereafter to welcome visitors. There is a kiln, the impressive mill itself, the stream from which the power was gleaned, and the millstones which ground the flour.

St. Kilda & Shiant Islands

Both islands are accessible via cruises from the Hebrides and the mainland, and are uninhabited by humans, except for some defense personnel and conservation workers in the summers. It is a UNESCO (United Nations Educational, Scientific and Cultural Organization) World Heritage Site for both natural and cultural reasons. There are two types of ancient sheep breeds remaining on the islands, the Soay (Neolithic) and Boreray (Iron Age). And while the islands are now uninhabited, there have been people here for at least two millennia, perhaps even four, as there is evidence of stone circles, cairns, and sheepfolds.

St. Kilda is the western-most point of the Outer Hebrides, and the largest island, Hirta, boasts the highest sea cliffs in the UK. There is no known saint associated with this island, but it's suggested the name St. Kilda is an Anglicized version of the Norse, *sunt kelda*, which translates to "sweet wellwater."

Shiant means "holy" or "enchanted," but whichever it is, these private islands are well-named. These are volcanic islands between Skye and Harris and have the dolerite columns similar to those in the Giant's Causeway in Ireland and Staffa, part of the Mull islands. The Shiant islands have large populations of seabirds, including puffins, guillemots, razorbills, fulmars, kittiwakes and skuas.

Ross and Cromarty: Mainland

Applecross Road

Until the 1970s, the Applecross Road, also known as the *Bealach nam Bò* (Pass of the Cattle), was the only road linking Applecross with the rest of the country. This twisting, single-track road reaches a height of two thousand and fifty-four feet, making it the third highest road in Scotland, and winds past the *Sgùrr a' Chaorachain*. The views are amazing, but be prepared for some precariously steep moments, as well as Alpine switchbacks and hairpin bends.

Castle Leod

Castle Leod

This keep is currently the clan seat of Clan MacKenzie and is owned (and occupied) by the current clan chief, the Earl of Cromartie. The castle dates from around the 15th century, though the date 1616 is carved of a dormer window in the extension.

This is rather small and compact, but renovated castle. It was very interesting to see the paintings of my forebears on the walls here, and to see the first real Ordnance map made of the area (by the English after Culloden in 1746, to keep the Scots in check). There is an enormous billiard table in one room, the room had been custom designed to fit it. The Victorian dining room still had panes of the original 17th century glass in it. There are a lot of Jacobite historical items on display, and even a little dungeon.

The Earl has a remarkable knowledge of history and family details. My great- grandmother was a McKenzie, so we were eager to explore this place.

The Clootie Well

This ancient custom is still in use throughout the British Isles. The term "clootie" comes from the Scottish "cloot" which means a strip of cloth. "Cloot" is possibly a corruption of the word "cloth." Clootie trees are almost always found beside a holy well. To make a wish, a cloot is dipped in the well water then tied to the tree while making a wish. It's disputed that if the wish is for healing, that the cloth be used to wash the affected part of the body in the holy water before tying to the tree. As the rag disintegrates, the wish gets sent into the world, or the ailment fades away. Both pagan shrines and holy wells have these traditions. There are many clootie trees and wells all over Scotland, but near Munlochy, there is a forested area with a particularly large Clootie Well on the south side of the road.

In Scotland, the arrival of the Roman church made holy well pilgrimages illegal, but it still continued in secret. This well is said to date back to circa 620 CE, where pilgrims would come, perform a ceremony by circling the well three times, clockwise, splash some water on the ground and make a prayer. Then they tied their cloth to a nearby tree. There are clootie trees all over Scotland, and indeed, Ireland and England as well. You may also see rosary beads, ribbons, and lengths of colorful yarn, but unfortunately, these days pranksters have been known to hang more than just strips of cloth, such as socks, ties, and even undergarments.

Corrieshalloch Gorge

Found twelve miles southeast of Ullapool, this spectacular gorge was formed in the last ice age. There is a Victorian bridge and a platform from which you can see the one-hundred-and-fifty-foot-high Falls of Measach. It is particularly dramatic after heavy rain, of course, and the falls usually produce a romantic mist along the gorge. Access is from the A832, on the south side of the gorge.

Crossing the bridge might be a challenge if you have a fear of heights, as it is two hundred feet high above the gorge. It sways a bit as you walk; but, if you can brave it, on the other side you can get to the viewing platform. Keep following the path west along the trees to reach another viewing platform, which sticks out halfway over the gorge. It is another test of those with a fear of heights, so be warned!

Take note that this site closes for repairs without notice.

Eagle Stone

Also known as *Clach an Tiompain*, this stone in Strathpeffer has a very clear carving of an eagle and a horseshoe-like arc symbol. Legend says it marks the place of a Scottish clan battle between Clan Munro and Clan

MacDonald in 1411, as the eagle is the symbol of the Munro Clan. The stone is associated with prophesies from the Brahan Seer, a 16th century prophet of the MacKenzie clan. He said that if the stone fell three times, the valley would be flooded. It has already fallen twice but is now anchored in concrete to prevent a third fall. Evidence shows the stone was originally down the hill near Dingwall, but it had been moved for unknown reasons to this location in 1411.

Edderton Cross Slab and *Clach Biorach*

A Class III Pictish stone, located in the old graveyard in Edderton village, this cross is made of stunning red sandstone. It has a simple Celtic cross on one side, and on the other side is a horseman with two riders below. This stone has recently been reset in the earth, as it had either sunk into the soil over the centuries, or the soil grew up around it. Either way, you will see a noticeable discoloration.

On the other side of Edderton village is the Edderton Symbol Stone, or *Clach Biorach*, a pillar of Bronze Age origin. This stone is nearly ten feet tall and is a Class I Pictish stone with double disc and salmon carvings.

Highland Museum of Childhood

Beginning life as a rural Victorian train station in Strathpeffer, this building houses toys and dolls which were originally in the private collection of Mrs. Angela Kellie. She donated the collection to the museum to tell the story of childhood in the Scottish Highlands. There are rocking horses, model yachts, marriage displays, a totem pole, and exhibits explaining various aspects of a child's life in the history of Scotland. Various themes such as birth and baptism, home life, leisure, child labor and education are portrayed, as well as several hands-on activities.

Inverewe Garden

As odd as it sounds, this is a botanical garden in the Highlands of Scotland. Located just north of Poolewe on a twenty-one-hundred-acre estate, the gardens themselves cover forty-nine acres. This garden was established by Osgood MacKenzie in 1862 after the land was gifted to him by his mother. He had originally built Inverewe Lodge, but it had been destroyed by fire in 1814 to be rebuilt in 1837 as Inverewe House. The garden began with some deer fencing and a dwarf willow in 1862, and now there are over twenty-five hundred exotic plants and flowers, as well as a huge rhododendron collection. A large, curved, walled garden has been reclaimed from the beach, and there are magnificent views across Loch Ewe.

The soil was originally acid and scarce, and not suitable for growing anything. However, determination reigned, and Osgood McKenzie worked his garden, bringing baskets of soil and trees. Over time, he transformed the rocky headland into the lush gardens they are today.

The estate was handed over to the National Trust for Scotland in 1952 by Osgood's daughter, Mairi Sawyer, along with a generous endowment for the gardens' upkeep.

Poolewe

While this was once a very important port town, and home to the Red Smiddy Iron Works, and a port of entry for cattle coming from Lewis and Harris via the ferry. Today, it is a charming village of white rendered buildings. The rustic St. Maelrubha's Church looks medieval but was built in 1965; it was dedicated to the 7th century monk who founded a monastery nearby and was the first Scottish Episcopal church to be built in the northwest Highlands since the Jacobite Revolution. There is also a dramatic War Memorial Celtic Cross overlooking Loch Ewe.

Stac Pollaidh

Anglicized to Stack Polly, this mountain has a rocky crest with pinnacles and gullies. *Stac Pollaidh* means "peak of the peat moss," and indeed, there is peat moss on the southern side. It is a popular climbing spot, with fine views and easy access via a modern road which leads to the large trail to the summit. It can be climbed in less than three hours by a relatively fit climber. If you are looking for a solitary climb, though, you will be disappointed, as the place is quite popular. Because this is such a popular climbing spot, the entire site has suffered from erosion, so take care while visiting.

There are some odd formations, such as the Lobster Claw Pinnacle, the Sphinx, the Tam o' Shanter and Andy Capp, to interest the photographers. The views of the Atlantic are incredible.

Roxburghshire

Jedburgh Abbey

The borders between Scotland and England have been contentious throughout the centuries, and Jedburgh Abbey is no exception. Established by David I in 1118 CE, the abbey has been subjected to attack and looting, and finally reduced to a parish church in 1560 with the coming of the Reformation. As the church started deteriorating, services moved into a small area of the nave in 1671 for safety reasons. It was finally abandoned in 1871 when a new church was built. By 1917, the site was handed over to Historic Scotland for care.

These ruins, while stripped of most decoration, are still beautiful and do retain some interesting features, such as the intricately carved fragment of a shrine that dates back to the 8th century. If you are a fan of delicate and intricate church architecture, this place will certainly not disappoint, with many colonnaded arcades and window casings, rose window, and the Romanesque main doorway. There is a model in the visitor's center of how the site may have looked in full repair.

Kelso Abbey

The grandest of the border abbeys, Kelso was founded during the reign of David I in 1128 by an order of Benedictines called Tironensians and took more than seventy- five years to complete. Kelso is a bit different in construction from other abbeys, as the choir and the nave each had a set of north and south transepts, and each had a tower over its crossing. The abbey was badly ruined in the Wars of Independence but was repaired. Later attacks in the 16th century occurred during the period of Rough Wooing, from which it never recovered. When the Reformation came in 1560, the Tironensian community was no longer recognized, and by 1587, the church was completely abandoned. Over the years, stones were removed and used to build structures elsewhere in the vicinity.

Melrose Abbey

There has been a monastery on this site since St. Aiden of Lindisfarne formed one in 650 CE. When the monastery was destroyed by Kenneth Mac Alpin in 839 CE, King David I reestablished the site in 1136 with monks from Rievaulx Abbey in Yorkshire, at which time, Melrose became the "mother church" of the order in Scotland. The abbey saw a number of attacks over the centuries but felt the sting of the Reformation. The final blow came during the Cromwellian War of the 1640s, also known as the English Civil War.

On this site is a marker where Robert the Bruce's embalmed heart, encased in lead, is buried. What makes this abbey remarkable is that it is reasonably intact, and still quite extensive.

Selkirkshire

Galashiels

There are several attractions in this town, including the Heriot-Watt University's School of Textiles and Design, and Galashiels Academy; the Old Gala House, a museum and art gallery with landscaped gardens; the war memorial with a massive sculpture of a Border Reiver horseman; and a ninety-mile Tweed Cycle Way cyclist trail. If you have an interest in Pictish works, there is an earthwork called the Picts' Work Ditch or Catrail, extending many miles south. An Iron Age fort and Torwoodlee Broch is on the northwest edge of town, though the structure was destroyed by the Romans.

Selkirk

There has likely been a settlement here since the 6th century, when the local Selgovae tribe converted to Christianity during the time of the Roman Empire's invasions of Caledonii. Selkirk is the site of the first Border Abbey, founded by Tironensians monks, however they soon moved to Kelso. The town flourished, despite the church's departure, and became known for its trade in textiles; townspeople today are still called Souters, which means cobblers, as Selkirk became a major hub for shoe-making. The improving economy saw a growing wool trade, as well. In spite of modern expansion and industry, the town center still retains its original medieval plan.

As the town expanded, it saw its share of history, including a royal castle erecting in 1301, known as Selkirk Peel; The church at Selkirk is where William Wallace was declared Guardian of the Kingdom of Scotland; and in 1799, Sir Walter Scott was appointed Sheriff-Deputy of the County of Selkirk, which was based in the Royal Burgh's Courthouse, now a museum.

If you are lucky enough to visit during the second Friday after the first Monday in June, you can witness one of the oldest ceremonies in the area. As many as four hundred riders participate in a cavalcade of the Selkirk Common Riding, running along the northern boundaries of the land. There is a week-long celebration around the event, including picnics, races, and festivals.

Yarrow Stone

Also known as the Liberalis Stone, it stands beside the track leading to Whitefield and just west of Yarrow. The stone has an early Christian inscription in Latin memorializing two British princes (Nudoss and Dumnogenus) who lived in the 5th and 6th centuries, which reads: *"This is the everlasting memorial. In this place lie the most famous princes Nudoss and Dumnogenus. In this tomb lie the two sons of Liberalis."*

The stone was discovered lying flat over some human remains. There were twenty cairns in the area, so it's a good area to explore if you've an interest in ancient burials or holy sites.

The Highlands

Shetland

Broch of Clickimin/Mousa Broch

A well-preserved broch on Shetland, this Pictish round structure stands on Clickimin Loch and is connected to the mainland with a stone causeway. One unusual feature is a stone slab with two sculptured footprints in the causeway. It was thought that footprints of that sort, like the one in Dunadd in Argyll, are associated with kingship.

You can explore the small Bronze Age farmhouse, the cattle enclosure, and the surrounding building foundations. This site was first occupied three thousand years ago, and the original settlement still has remains. The tower itself is also called Mousa Broch, and once stood about sixteen yards high. There are some five hundred brochs in Scotland, and the Boch of Mousa is probably the most well-preserved broch of them all, however Clickimin is more accessible.

Byre Chapel

Byre Chapel is a church that doesn't look like a church! This byre (cowshed or barn) has been converted into a small chapel, while retaining its original features. The interior is simple and beautiful, with hay bales, wooden pews and cross, and a simple concrete floor decorated with a crisscross pattern. The pews are covered with sheepskins for comfort. It was originally the chapel of the Society of Our Lady of the Isles, a convent that has now been moved to a purpose-built chapel nearby.

Fair Isle

By definition, this is a hidden place. It is the most remote inhabited island in the UK, and measures three by one-and-a-half miles. It is the southernmost island of the Shetland Islands, and it is halfway to the Orkney group. Fair Isle is most known for the bird observatory, and for its traditional style of knitting.

This place has been inhabited since the Bronze Age, with a current occupancy of sixty-eight (as of the 2013 census) who live on crofts in the south. You can observe workers while they build boats, spin, weave, or knit. While there are no pubs or restaurants on the island, there is a permanent bird observatory, founded by George Waterston in 1948 and provides catered accommodation, rather than hostelry.

Doune
Castle

Jarlshof

This is the best known prehistoric archeological site on Shetland, located near the southern tip of the main island, dating from 2,500 BCE through the 17th century. The Bronze Age settlers built several oval houses that are mostly underground, but excavated, as well as a smithy; Iron Age settlers created a broch and defensive walls; Picts added several works of art, wheelhouses, and a symbol stone; Viking ruins include a longhouse and a medieval farmhouse.

You will see several layers of civilization in this one place. Stone Age, Bronze Age, Iron Age, Pictish, Norse, and Medieval artifacts and buildings are on location, and each one offers a different glimpse into the past. If you normally skip over the explaining exhibit signs to just enjoy the actual artifacts, you may miss some of the wonder and awe this site has to offer, so take some time to learn about what you are seeing first.

Stirlingshire

Balquhidder

Founded by St Angus in the 8th or 9th century, it is known as a magical place, called a Thin Place by the Celts, where the place between Heaven and Earth meets. St. Angus blessed the glen at the house *Beannach Aonghais* (Blessing of Angus) is now located, and there is a small stone oratory at Kirkton, where he lived.

Balquhidder village has lovely mountain terrain and is home to the MacGregor Clan. 18th century folk hero and outlaw, Robert Roy MacGregor, known more familiarly as Rob Roy, lived and died here. The ruins of the small cottage where he lived while under the protection of John Campbell, 2nd Duke of Argyll, can be found in Glen Shira. His remains, along with those of his wife and son, can be found in the Balquhidder graveyard.

Bar Hill Roman Fort & Antonine Wall

Built circa 143 CE, this small ruin is what remains of the highest fort on the Antonine Wall, the secondary largest boundary past Hadrian's Wall. There is a small Iron Age fort to the east, and the wall ditch runs past both. It is one of two places to get the best view of the wall and its surrounding area and includes baths as well as the fort.

The wall was thirty-seven miles long, and cut the country in half, dividing the Highlands from the Lowlands, but it was only in use for about twenty years. Rough Castle is the other good spot to explore the wall and is just two miles west of Falkirk. This castle is the smallest of the nineteen fortlets built along the wall, and the best preserved.

Sutherland

Doune Castle

This site had probably been a fort in Roman times, but the castle itself was originally built in the 13th century by the Stewart family, and has been used since as a hunting lodge, dower house, and royal retreat. It was used as a prison and garrison in the 17th and 18th centuries after the Earls of Moray, the Stuarts, took possession in the 16th century.

While much of it is a ruin, the castle is in remarkable shape, and many rooms have been fully restored to allow visitors. The hall is vaulted and, unusually, features double fireplaces. Take some time to see the Lord's Tower, the Great Hall and Kitchen Tower, courtyard and curtain walls, and enjoy the stunning scenery.

Falkirk Wheel

The world's only rotating boat lift, this fascinating engineering feat is worth a look, even if you aren't a transport or engineering enthusiast. There is a particular elegance to this odd structure. Opened in 2002, it connects the Forth and Clyde Canal with the Union Canal. It replaces eleven locks and is quite spectacular and a little surreal to see in operation. Inspirations for the design include the double-headed Celtic Axe, a ship's propeller, and even a whale's ribcage.

Kelpie Sculpture

Just completed in September 2013, these two massive sculptures are ninety- eight feet high and situated above the Forth & Clyde canal, forming a dramatic gateway. Designed by sculptor Andy Scott, the Kelpies (water horses, or Each Uisge) are a monument to the heritage of horse-powered industry across central Scotland.

They are definitely impressive sculptures, and in the right light, they reflect on the water of the canal, making for a fantastic photo opportunity. The legend of the kelpie is listed in the History and Myths section of this book.

Sango Bay

Muiravonside Graveyard

The high percentage of elaborately carved gravestones in this 18th century graveyard are mostly due to one stonemason, who evidently enjoyed his work very much. The carvings along the edges of the stones include skulls, heads, angels and mortals, crossed bones, hourglasses, castles, trumpet motifs, and more. The details are amazing, intricate, and worth a long visit to explore all the unusual art, especially as gravestones typically are left to decay over time. These are in remarkably well-preserved states.

Sutherland

Ardvreck Castle

Looking like a stone hand coming up out of the land, this lonely, ruined castle on Loch Assynt, along the northern coast of Scotland, dates from the 16th century, though the MacLeods owned surrounding lands since the 13th century. MacLeod ownership was short-lived, however, as it was captured by the MacKenzie Clan in 1672, who also took control of the surrounding lands. The MacKenzies built the nearby Calda House in 1726, but it burned down in 1737 under mysterious circumstances, and remains in ruin today.

The castle is deceptively small, but was originally a large, imposing structure which included a walled garden. There is also a vaulted cellar below. Only the ground floor is accessible, but be mindful, as the loch is tidal and will quickly flood the causeway to the island.

The castle is said to be haunted by two ghosts. One is a tall man dressed in gray and may be the Marquis of Montrose. The other ghost is a young girl, who had been betrothed to a MacKenzie as payment to build the castle. She despaired and threw herself off the tower. There is also a mermaid or selkie legend associated with the loch.

Visitors have claimed to see strange lights from the castle, while others at the castle have claimed seeing what look like car headlights at dusk and waited, but no car appeared.

Baile an Or

Derived from the Norse word Hjalmundal, meaning Dale of the Hamlet, the town of Helmsdale gained its biggest notoriety from the Great Sutherland Gold Rush of 1868. Two tributaries of River Helmsdale saw the greatest success during the gold rush, at the Suisgill and Kildonan burns. Who doesn't want to go find gold? There is a small information center on Suisgill Estate, where you can sign up to go gold panning (though don't expect to strike it rich!), camp free of charge, or just enjoy the surrounding beauty of the Highlands.

Clachtoll Broch

Though heavily ruined, this broch still boasts the double-wall construction common with this type of fort, as well as the stairway running up through the space between the walls. It has a huge triangular lintel stone above its doorway, as well as lintels on the cells and wall chambers. It is considered one of the most spectacular Iron Age settlements in the northwest area of Scotland. It sits on a rocky outcrop on the Bay of Clachtoll, with views across the bay to the village of Stoer. As you approach, it doesn't look like much, perhaps just a tumbled pile of rocks, but as you round the front, it forms an organized structure.

Dunrobin
Castle

Dunrobin Castle, Gardens, and Museum

If you think this castle looks like it belongs in a fairy tale, you'd be right. Originally dating from the 1300s, it has been rebuilt and added onto several times over the centuries. It has turrets and towers, sweeping staircases, and manicured gardens, which were inspired by the palace at Versailles. Overlooking the waters of Dornoch Firth, you will see the formal gardens from the balconies, and the sea lies just beyond. It is a glittering sight to behold! You can also watch a falconry demonstration if you get there at the right time.

It is definitely worth a tour, as the rooms are all beautifully preserved. One is full of period clothing, ball gowns, and uniforms. Portraits adorn many walls. Needlework from the 5th Duke's wife is in the paneled dining room. And the Library boasts more than ten thousand books. The museum is full of trophy heads from many animals shot by family members while on safari, as well as displays of archaeological artifacts discovered on the estate.

Dunrobin Castle

Sandwood Bay

Having been called the most magnificent beach in the UK, it is an isolated, picturesque mile-long beach that lies to the south of Durness and Cape Wrath.

Sandwood probably gets its name from the Norse word *Sandvatn*, meaning sand water. It's believed Norse longships were dragged across the dunes here to Sandwood Loch. Today, you will find a mile-and-a-half of pinkish sand and huge sand dunes. Sea cliffs and an impressive sea stack face right into the fierce North Atlantic Ocean. It is not easy to get to, but that is part of why it is so unspoiled.

There is a public road a few miles northwest of Kinlochbervie. The walk is about four miles long, and isn't the most interesting stroll, but the result is worth it. There is peat bog on either side, so don't stray from the path.

There are several legends of this remote beach, including the sighting of a yellow-tailed mermaid, and the ghost of a mariner, victim of a shipwreck off the coast, said to knock on the windows of the old cottage near the beach when it was still inhabited. This stretch of coastline has been a host to numerous shipwrecks over the centuries, all of which lay out at sea, or indeed under the sand.

West Lothian

Almond Castle

Approach this ruined castle with care, as the walls are not maintained and can crumble. It would be much safer to view from the outside. Also called The Haining and Haining Castle, this structure likely dates back to the early 15th century. It passed into the Livingston family in 1542 by way of marriage and underwent some expansion in later decades. After several generations, the current lord, Sir James Livingston, was given the title of Lord Almond, after which the castle adopted the name Almond. It has been a ruin since this Lord backed the Jacobite movement, and had his lands forfeited to the crown. Perhaps one day this lovely ruin will be restored… carefully.

Blackness Castle

This 15th century fortress has an odd, defensive shape which follows the contours of the rocky coastline of the shore of the Firth of Forth. Originally built in the mid-15th century by Sir George Crichton, this castle served as the main port serving the Royal Burgh of Linlithgow. The lands and titles were forfeited to the crown at the time of King James II of Scotland, and it has remained in crown hands ever since. It has been a state prison, garrison, and ammunition depot. In the mid-16th century, the castle was one of the most advanced artillery fortifications in Scotland at the time. Still, it fell to Cromwell's army in 1650. It was briefly occupied during World War I but has largely been abandoned ever since. It is now in the care of Historic Scotland. It's been called the "ship that never sailed," due to its odd shape and position on the Forth.

Five Sisters Zoo

You've been tramping around churches and castles, so you need a place to take the kids, and run off some pent-up energy. This rescue and rehabilitation center is a great place to take the kids for a day out. There are animals, birds, and reptiles from all over the world. You can even become a zookeeper for a half or full day, or a half day for kids six to sixteen where the day's chores include cleaning pens, feeding the animals, learning to handle the various species. At the end of the day, your child receives a certificate of zookeeping and a gift. Other activities include a play castle and pirate ship area. If you get hungry, there is the Brown Bear Café for some sandwiches or soups, or box lunches for the kids.

Linlithgow Palace

This palace is an imposing structure on a picturesque loch, a fantastic place to see a magnificent great hall, fountains, angel musician sculptures, and beautiful, elegant windows. The palace was a principal royal residence for Scottish monarchs of the 15th and 16th centuries. The last major event that took place there was when Bonnie Prince Charlie visited in September 1745, when the fountains were said to have flowed with wine. Four short months later, the castle saw its destruction by the army of the Duke of Cumberland in 1746. It has since been partially restored and is now open to the public. It is said to be haunted by the ghost of Mary of Guise, mother of Mary, Queen of Scots.

Wigtownshire

Barsalloch Fort

This two-thousand-year-old fortified farmstead has never been excavated but was likely lived in by a tribe the Romans called the Novantae. It is on the edge of a sea cliff, with views of the Isle of Man, Northern Ireland, and the Mull of Galloway. There are earthen ramparts and probably contained at least two large roundhouses, possibly four, and irregular in shape. Great for rambling exploration, as you imagine the possibilities.

Drumtroddan Stones

This is really two sites; one is an alignment of three stones (one fallen), and the other is a set of rocks marked with cup and ring carvings. They are located between Port William and Whithorn. The first site dates to circa 2000 BCE, with stones about ten feet tall. The nearby cup and ring stones are reached through a farmstead and were probably carved during the Bronze Age. It's possible that they were aligned with the midsummer sunrise in the northwest, and the midwinter sunset in the southwest. They are on a large open plateau, surrounded by a small stone wall, offering safety and isolation.

Logan Botanic Gardens

Because this southwest tip of Scotland has a mild climate, there are many trees and plants that wouldn't normally survive outdoors in Scotland. It has a Woodland Garden, a Walled Garden, a Water Garden, and a Terrace Garden with Chusan palms. Walk along the pond within the Walled Garden, explore what little remains of Castle Balzieland, and stroll through the fifty varieties of eucalyptus. It is open April through September.

Isle of Skye

CONCLUSION

I do hope you enjoyed your journey through the Lowlands, Highlands, and Islands of Scotland. The land is so enriched by history, legend, and myth, a stunning jewel on the crown of Europe. There is a passion of place and people in this land, strong and deep, though sometimes its austere and silent as well. It is manifest in the manner of the people, the strength of the hills, and the beauty in the art and architecture.

If you travel anywhere, it helps, I believe, to have some sense of history, some knowledge of the myths and beliefs of the land. I believe this increases the magic the land reflects into the true traveler. Whether you are visiting to enjoy the beautiful gardens, the charming pubs, the hidden magic places, the stunning architecture, or the megalithic monuments of Scotland, you will not be disappointed. It is a place to hold dear; a place to make memories to treasure and relish; a stunning place of magic and mystery.

Yearning to delve into the mysteries of the Emerald Isle? Skip the tourist traps and unearth new ways to delight in its legendary landscape.

Ireland: Mythical, Magical, Mystical: A Guide to Hidden Ireland is an eye-opening travel guidebook. If you like escaping the beaten path, a conversational approach, and creating lasting memories, then you'll love Christy Nicholas's invaluable resource.

Start reading **Ireland: Mythical, Magical, Mystical: A Guide to Hidden Ireland** and delve into your dream trip today!

From dreams to desperation.
When the magical secrets of The Emerald Isle beckon, can she discover her destiny?

Legacy of Hunger is the sweeping first book in The Druid's Brooch historical fantasy series. If you like determined female characters, immersive authenticity, and a wee touch of fairy magic, then you'll love Christy Nicholas's transatlantic adventure.

Start reading **Legacy of Hunger** to trace a family treasure today!

THANK YOU!

Thank you so much for enjoying this guide. If you've enjoyed the story, please consider leaving a review so other readers can discover Scotland's hidden treasures!

If you would like to get updates, sneak previews, sales, and contests, please sign up for my newsletter.

GreenDragonArtist.com/about/newsletter/

**See all the books available
through Green Dragon Publishing at
GreenDragonArtist.com/Books**

MAPS AND RESOURCES

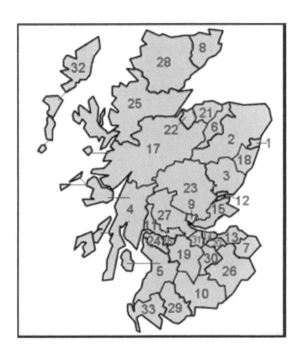

WEBSITE RESOURCES

General Scotland Information

Green Dragon Artist, http://www.greendragonartist.com, my own website dedicated to travel in the UK.

Undiscovered Scotland, http://www.undiscoveredscotland.co.uk – fantastic interactive map and information resource.

Scotland, — A great resource for all things Scottish.

Mythical, Mystical, Historical or Hidden Places

Celtic Myth Podshow, https://podcasts.apple.com/us/podcast/celtic-myth-podshow/id272848127 — dramatizations of Celtic myths.

Orkneyjar, http://www.orkneyjar.com/ — the heritage of the Orkney Islands.

Powerful Places, http://www.powerfulplaces.com — a great set of books and a blog for spiritual places in the British Isles.

Sacred Texts, http://www.sacred-texts.com – a guide to tales from William Yeats, Lady Gregory and many others.

Stone Pages, http://www.stonepages.com — a guide to stone circles and standing stones.

Thin Place, http://www.thinplace.net — a guide to spiritual places.

UNESCO World Heritage Centre, http://whc.unesco.org — listing of World Heritage sites.

Travel Related Sites

Auto Europe, https://www.autoeurope.com/ — Car Rental.

Enterprise Car Rental, http://www.enterprise.com.

Expedia, http://www.expedia.com.

Fodor's Forums, http://www.fodors.com/community — great help (and some snarky advice) from others who have been there.

Google Maps, https://maps.google.com.

Green Traveller, http://www.greentraveller.co.uk — for those that prefer low carbon holidays.

Insure My Trip, — to compare travel insurance plans.

Listed properties of the UK, http://www.list.co.uk.

Scotrail, http://www.scotrail.co.uk.

Scottish pubs, http://www.insiders-scotland-guide.com/ScottishPubs.html.

Seat Guru, — find out which seats are best.

Slow Travel, https://www.smartertravel.com/art-slow-travel — for those who wish to travel at a slower pace.

Traditional Music and Song, http://www.tmsa.org.uk.

Trip Advisor, — for researching the B&Bs, hotels, and sites.

Via Michelin, — great for planning routes and times.

Unusual places to stay, http://www.quirkyaccom.com.

Discount Sources

Airfare Watchdog, — for discount airfare.

Edinburgh Pass, http://www.edinburgh.org/pass.

Flyertalk, — for those who travel frequently.

Historic Scotland Pass, http://www.historic-scotland.gov.uk/explorer.htm.

Kayak, http://www.kayak.com.

Last Minute Travel, — for last-minute airfare deals.

Lonely Planet, — good all-round site, especially for tight budgets.

National Heritage Membership, http://www.britainexpress.com/scotland/index.html.

STA Travel, – for student and teacher travel.

Student Universe, — for student and teacher travel.

Travel Zoo, — for discount airfare.

Veteran's Advantage, — for veteran travel.

Photography Sources

DP Review, – to compare cameras.

Lulu, – for book and calendar printing.

Simply Canvas, – for photographic printing.

White House Custom Copies, – for photographic printing.

Print Resources

- Ashmore, P.J., Neolithic and Bronze Age Scotland: An Authoritative and Lively Account of an Enigmatic Period of Scottish Prehistory, Batsford, 2003.
- Campbell, John Gregorson, The Gaelic Otherworld, Birlinn, Ltd., 2012.
- Herman, A., How the Scots Invented the Modern World, Crown Publishing Group, 2001.
- Hunter, James, Last of the Free; A History of the Highlands and Islands of Scotland, Mainstream Publishing, 2000.
- MacDonald, Charles, Moidart Among the Clanranalds, Birlinn, Ltd., 2011.
- MacDonald, Donald, Tales and Traditions of the Lews, Birlinn, Ltd., 2000.
- Mackie, J.D., A History of Scotland, Pelican, 1964.
- Marwick, Ernest, The Folklore of Orkney and Shetland, Birlinn, Ltd., 1975.
- Matthews, John. Celtic Myths and Legends, Pitkin Guides, 2001. McNeill, F. Marian, The Silver Bough, Canongate, 2001.

- Paterson, Raymond Campbell, The Lord of the Isles: A History of Clan Donald, Birlinn, Ltd., 2008.
- Pryor, F., Britain B.C.: Life in Britain and Ireland before the Romans, Harper Collins, 2003.
- Scott, Ronald McNair, Robert the Bruce, King of Scots, Canongate, 1996.
- Sjoestedt, Marie-Louise. Gods and Heroes of the Celts. London, 1949. Translation by Miles Dillon of Sjoestedt's Dieux et hèros des Celtes. Paris, 1940.
- Stewart, R.J. Celtic Gods, Celtic Goddesses. Blandford Press, 1992.
- Stewart, R.J. Celtic Myths, Celtic Legends. Blandford Press, 1996.
- Sykes, Bryan, Saxons, Vikings and Celts: The Genetic Roots of Britain and Ireland, W.W. Norton & Company, 2007.

APPENDIX

Gaelic, unless otherwise noted (pronunciation guide), **English name and definition.**

(Note, Irish and Scottish Gaelic are similar in many ways, but they are separate. Many of the phrases and names listed here are shared between the two cultures)

Aethelstane (AYTH-el-stane), A Saxon King.

Alt Clut (alt cloot), A kingdom of the Picts.

Am Fear Liath Mòr (am FAR LEE-ah more), The Big Grey Man of Ben MacDhui.

An Dubh Sgeir (an doov skeer), A sea stack in the Duirinish peninsula of the Isle of Skye.

An Stac (an stack), A sea stack in the Duirinish peninsula of the Isle of Skye.

Aos-sìdhe (as SHEE), Fairy folk.

Athfhinn (AH-een), The Very Bright One, wife of Fionn mac Cumhaill.

Balor (BAY-lor) of the Evil Eye – A king of the Fomorians.

Bealach nam Bò (BEE-lakh nam bow), Pass of the Cattle.

Beannach Aonghais (BAN-nakh AYNG-us), Blessing of Angus, a small house in Balquhidder.

Bean-Nighe (ban nee), Washer Woman, or a fairy omen of death.

Bean-Sìdhe (ban shee), Fairy Woman, or a fairy omen of death.

Beli (BELL-ee), Also known as Belenus, the "Fair Shining One," he was a god of the fire or the sun.

Benandonner (BEN-an-don-er), Suitor of Fionn mac Cumhaill's sweetheart.

Bodach (BOW-dakh), Old man.

Brùnaidh/Gruagach/Ùruisg (BROO-nee/GROO-ah-gakh/OO-risk), A good natured brownie elf or house goblin.

Caerinii (CAYR-ee-nee), A Celtic tribe (the sheep folk).

Càillèach (KAHL-ee-akh), Cailleach, or Hag, a goddess who brings the winter.

Càillèach Bheur (KAHL-ee-akh voor), The Winter Goddess.

Càillèach Bheur's Clacharan (KAHL-ee-akh voors CLACK-ah-ran), Stepping stones of the winter goddess.

Calanais (call-a-NISH), Callanish, a stone circle on the Isle of Lewis.

Cat Sìdhe (cat shee), Fairy Cat.

Catuvallanii (CAT-oo-vall-a-nee), A Latin name for a Celtic tribe, People of the Cat.

Ceann Mòr (kyan more), Great Chief (literally, "large head").

Ceasg (kesk), A mermaid, also known as *maighdean mhara* (maid of the sea).

Cèilidh (KAY-lee), A party.

Cìnaed mac Ailpìn (Kenneth McAlpin), The first king of Scotland.

Clach an Tiompain (clack an TEEM-payn), Eagle Stone, a Pictish stone. *Clach an t'Sagairt* (clack an TAG-art), The Priest's Stone, a Pictish stone.

Clach Ard (clack ard), Tall Stone, a Pictish stone.

Clach Biorach (clack BEE-oh-rakh), Sharp Stone, a Pictish stone.

Clàrsach (KLAR-sakh), Scottish harp.

Cockermay Doucri (COCK-er-may DOO-kree), David the Foundling, an abandoned child adopted by Saint William of Perth.

Coirebhreacain (COR-eh-vree-kayn), Cauldron of the Plaids.

Colm Cille (KOL-um khill), St. Columba, "Dove of the Church," who brought Christianity to Scotland from Ireland.

Conneach Odhar (CONN-eekh OW-er), The Brahan Seer, a prophet of the McKenzie clan.

Cranachan (CRAN-a-khan), A traditional dessert with raspberries, toasted oats, cream, honey and sometimes whisky.

Crùachan Feli (Kroo-ah-kan FAY-lee), The Mountain of Ireland.

Cù Chulainn (KOO khoo-lann)/Cuchulain), A hero, son of Lugh and *Deichtine*. (DEEKH-tee-neh), originally named *Sètanta* (say-TAHN-tah).

Cù Sìdhe (koo shee), Fairy Dog.

Cuingealach (KOON-gay-lakh), Narrow place.

Dagda (DAG-dah), A Celtic god, known as the "good" god, a father god.

Dàl Riata (doll ree-AH-tah), A tribe of Irish Celts that came to Scotland. *Damnonii* (DAM-no-nee), A Latin name for a Celtic tribe.

Danù (DAH-noo), A Celtic goddess, the mother goddess.

Daoine Sìth (DIN-ay shee), People of Peace, a name for the fairies.

Dauphin (dow-FAN), The heir to the French throne.

Domhbnall Dubh (DOVE-nall doov), Black Donald, the devil *Dùn* (dun), A fort.

Dunadd (DOON-add), A fortress of the *Fortriù* tribe.

Dyn Barr (dun bar), Fort of the Point (in Brythonic).

Each Uisge (EEKH ISH-gay), Water horse or kelpie.

Epona (eh-PONE-ah), A Celtic horse goddess, *Epos* in Gaulish, *Eqvos* in Old Celtic.

Epidii (eh-PEED-eye), A Latin name for a Celtic tribe.

Fachan (FAKH-ahn), Peg Leg Jack, a frightening creature of legend.

Fionn mac Cumhaill (FINN mack KOOWOL)/Finn MacCool. The leader of the Fianna, guardians of Ireland, also known as Fingal.

Fortriù (FOR-tree-oo), A kingdom of the Picts.

Galdus (GALL-dus), A mythical Scottish king.

Ghillie Dhu (GHILL-ee doo), A solitary elf, guardian of trees.

Glaistig (GLASS-teeg), A spirit who cares for livestock.

Gruagach (GROO-ah-gakh), A ghost associated with the fortunes of a particular family.

Hungus (HUN-gus), A Pictish king.

Jacobus (JACK-oh-bus), The Latin name for James, from which came the name for the Jacobite Revolution.

Leanan Sìdhe (LEE-nan shee), Fairy Lover.

Lìr (LEER), Irish sea god.

Lochan na Cailliche (LOCK-an nah KAHL-ee-akh), Lake of the winter goddess.

Lù/Lugh (LOO), A man of the Tuatha dè Danann, noted for his many gifts *Macha* (MAHK-ah), A mother goddess of the *Tuatha dè Danann.*

Màel Colùm I (Malcolm I), A Scottish king.

Màel Colùm mac Cinàeda (Malcolm II), A Scottish king.

Màel Coluim III (Malcolm III), A Scottish king.

Manannàn mac Lìr (mah-NAN-an mak leer), Irish sea god, also known as *Manau* or *Mannan.*

Morrigan (MOR-i-gahn), A goddess of war, fertility and horses.

Nèl (NEEL), A Spartan commander, husband of the Egyptian Scota

Nighean (NEE-han), Daughter.

Novantae (NO-van-tay), A Latin name for a Celtic tribe.

Nuadha Airgetlàmh (noo-AH-tha AYR-get-lav), Nuada of the Silver Arm, the first king of the *Tuatha dè Danaan.*

Òengus mac Fergusa (ANG-us mack fer-GOOS-ah), A Pictish King in the 8th Century.

Oisìn (OY-shin), Ossian, an Irish poet, a member of the Fianna, and son of *Fionn mac Cumhaill.*

Pherath (FER-ah), A Pictish king.

Pìob Mhòr (Peeb vor), Great Highland Bagpipes.

Pìobaireachd (PEE-bar-eekh), The traditional music for bagpipes, also known as *cèol mòr,* or great music.

Protocletos, The Greek name for Saint Andrew.

Puirt a' bhèil (pert ah VEEL), Literally, "mouth music", A type of rhythmic, a capella song designed to be sung while doing boring tasks, like waulking wool.

Scàthach (SKATH-ack), A warrior woman who runs a school on the Isle of Skye.

Scotii (SKOT-ee), A Latin name for an Irish tribe of Celts who migrated to Scotland.

Seonaidh (SHAW-nee), A water spirit who would leave you alone if you gave it ale.

Sgùrr a' Chaorachain (sgoor ah KOW-ra-khayn), A mountain in Applecross.

Sluagh Sìdhe (SLOO-ah shee), The Fairy Host.

Smertae (SMER-tay), A Latin name for a Celtic tribe.

Taranis (TAR-ah-neesh), A Celtic thunder god.

Teàrlach (TCHAR-lokh), Gaelic for Charles, where the term Bonnie Prince Charlie came from.

Tigh na Cailliche (tee nah KAHL-ee-akh), A small stone house in Glen Lyon dedicated to the winter goddess, the Càillèach.

Tigh nà Ruaich (tee nah ROO-akh), The House of the Heather.

Tuatha dè Danaan (TOO-a-ha day DAH-nan), Race of Fairies in Irish folklore.

Uisge Bàn (ISH-kee bahn), Fair Water.

Uisce Beatha (ISH-kee BAH-ha), Whisky, the Water of Life.

Veniconea (VEN-i-cone-ee), A Latin name for a Celtic tribe.

Wudewas (WOOD-e-was), Woodmen in Gaulish.

DEDICATION

I would like to dedicate this book to my parents, D. Paul and Judy. My love of art and travel, as well as my sense of determination comes directly from them, and I love them deeply for it. I would also like to thank my supportive husband, Jason, without whom I would be lost and adrift.

ABOUT THE AUTHOR

Christy Nicholas writes under several pen names, including Rowan Dillon, CN Jackson, and Emeline Rhys. She's an author, artist, and accountant. After she failed to become an airline pilot, she quit her ceaseless pursuit of careers that began with the letter 'A' and decided to concentrate on her writing. Since she has Project Completion Compulsion, she is one of the few authors with no unfinished novels.

Christy has her hands in many crafts, including digital art, beaded jewelry, writing, and photography. In real life, she's a CPA, but having grown up with art all around her (her mother, grandmother, and great-grandmother are/were all artists), it infected her, as it were. She wants to expose the incredible beauty in this world, hidden beneath the everyday grime of familiarity and habit, and share it with others. She uses characters out of time and places infused with magic and myth, writing magical realism stories in both historical fantasy and time travel flavors.

Social Media Links:
Blog: www.GreenDragonArtist.net
Website: www.GreenDragonArtist.com
Facebook: www.facebook.com/greendragonauthor
Instagram: www.instagram.com/greendragonartist9
TikTok: www.tiktok.com/@greendragonauthor